ENCHANTMENT IS

Goin' to the chapel?
For a marriage spell, use as directed, one orange, spring water, rose water (or maple syrup), nutmeg, rice and one whole coconut for seven nights, while chanting "I do, I do, I do."

Keep your car safe.
Try mink oil, dried cranberries, mustard seeds, a zipper food storage bag, and rice or dried corn or wheat germ.

Believe it or not, garlic is an aphrodisiac.
Roasted garlic with fresh basil leaves and plum tomatoes can be served to a shy date to make him more active.

Dream a little dream and cure your insomnia.
Eat three slices of turkey, drink chamomile tea or hot milk, and place nutmeg and oregano under your pillow to prevent nightmares.

Ditch your unwanted guests.
Launder their clothes in a solution of detergent, vinegar, red pepper, and stain remover and shout their name three times followed by the word "OUT!"

The Supermarket Sorceress

Lexa Roséan

St. Martin's Paperbacks

THE SUPERMARKET SORCERESS

Copyright © 1996 by St. Martin's Press.

Cover photograph by Herman Estévez.

ISBN: 0-312-95768-8

Printed in the United States of America

St. Martin's Paperbacks trade paperback edition/March 1996

St. Martin's Paperbacks are published by St. Martin's Press.

10 9 8 7 6 5 4 3 2 1

This book is dedicated in loving memory
to my mother, Malkah Schatzman,
who took me to my first supermarket
and instilled in me my belief in magic.

NOTE TO READER

While the spells and enchantments which follow use commonly available ingredients, if you have any allergies or sensitivities to a particular ingredient, refrain from attempting that spell. Heed all warnings and instructions on the products you use.

CONTENTS

CONTENTS

INTRODUCTION

Welcome to the world of supermarket sorcery. The goal of this book is to create a magical bridge between the ancient and modern worlds; to reveal the powerful secrets still hidden in seemingly everyday products. Magic is a form of prayer, a way to petition the gods. Witches believe that the gods' divine spark is present in everything on the planet. Their energies are always at work and those energies can be harnessed for good or evil.

For instance, every food product is ruled by a planet or astrological sign, just as is every person. Some foods have historical or magical connections with specific deities. It is this information that can guide us in how to utilize each food's magical properties. These attributes are as real as the nutritional values that foods contain. For example, no one questions the fact that leeks are a source of iron; in the same way, the ancient soldiers of Wales never questioned the fact that leeks would bring them success in battle. All of these spells are based on legend, lore, historical, and astrological information about products. Some products are suggested as modern equivalents for ancient and hard to obtain items.

In my fourteen years of experience as a psychic, witch, and high priestess, I have counseled people from many walks of life. One thing many of them had in common was an awe of the powers of witch-craft. They felt an attraction and a fear at the same time, or felt they were breaking some taboo or experimenting with the powers of evil. This is a misconception about witchcraft created primarily by the fathers of the Medieval Inquisition and perpetuated by Hollywood. According to Charlie Murphy, a pagan folklorist, "nine million European women died" during the 500 year reign of the Inquisition. Terror was employed to force public acceptance of the church, and the Goddess along with her priestesses were systematically demonized.

It is interesting to note that Shakespeare's source for the witches in *Macbeth* was Holinshed's *Chronicles,* in which the entities who spoke to Macbeth were described as the three Fates, or beautiful fairies or nymphs. Shakespeare changed them into ugly old hags. Somehow the positive image of the Divine Feminine has been lost and replaced by the image of an old, long-nosed witch with a pointed hat and warts on her chin. The modern movement of Wicca, a reconstructionalist matriarchal religion, is desperately fighting to change that image. Modern witches are now being seen as healers and beautiful people made in the image of the God and Goddess.

Spells and magic are gifts of knowledge passed down from generation to generation by shamans who understood the ways of the Earth and how to utilize the herbs and foods that grew upon it. This brings me to another misconception about magic and spells: Many people are interested in doing spells to attract health, love, money, and success into their lives but they think the ingredients for these spells are too difficult to obtain.

> Double, double, toil and trouble;
> Fire burn, and cauldron bubble.
> Eye of newt and toe of frog,
> Wool of bat and tongue of dog.

Oh, that Shakespeare!

In defense of the witches of old, many of these "scarier" terms are simply nicknames for herbs and plants. There is some discrepancy over whether eye of newt is truly the eye of a salamander or simply a type of marsh berry. Tongue of dog is most definitely the common term for wild vanilla leaf. It is also known as deer's tongue, because deer are constantly munching on this particular grass. But you will not have to go out in a meadow to pick fresh herbs; you can simply stroll down aisle five in your supermarket. In this modern day and age, if a spell called for tongue of dog you would pick up a vanilla bean or vanilla extract. The ingredients for all the recipes in this spell book can be obtained easily in your local supermarket.

A word about intent: The witches creed is "Do what thou wilt and ye harm none," similar to the Judeo/Christian Golden Rule, "Do unto others as you would have them do unto you." Magic should not be used to manipulate others against their will. This is considered black magic. It is best to keep the focus on ourselves and our own needs. For instance, we can do a love spell to try and force someone into liking us (these spells usually backfire) or we can do a love spell with the intent of drawing love into our lives and trust the gods to lead us toward the person who will realize our desires.

As experience has taught me not to bludgeon people over the head to do "the right thing," I have included some spells of a manipulatory nature (see Enemies section and Fidelity and Infidelity section). In such cases I have also included the spells that counteract them or spells of a different nature. For example in the enemy section, you can do a spell to freeze your enemy or you can choose the spell to let go of unpleasant feelings. The choice is yours. Let your conscience be your guide. Witchcraft is not a religion of rules and sins, rewards and punishments. It is a spiritual path involving the pursuit of the divine connection within. In "The Charge of the Goddess," an anonymous litany from the witches' book of shadows, the Goddess says: "Learn this mystery . . . if what thou seekest thou findeth not within thee, thou wilt never find it without thee. For behold . . . I have been with thee from the beginning, and I am that which is to be attained at the end of desire."

The real power lies within you. All spells in this book are simply tools and symbols to aid in your own empowerment. Remember, magic is best done with reverence, humility, and a healthy sense of humor! Good luck and good magic.

ACKNOWLEDGMENTS

Thanks to: my agent, Sandra Martin, for making this book possible; my editor, Jennifer Enderlin, for her patience and faith in me; Diane Sinclair, for her expertise in law and cooking lamb; Sally Sockwell, for her New Testament research; my sisters, Bracha and Randyl, and my father, A. L. Roséan, for their input and support. My deepest love and thanks to Carol Bulzone and Enchantments, Mallory Loehr, Claire Olivia Moed, and the Dorjanda family.

MOON PHASES

There are three basic phases of the moon: new, full, and dark. They correspond to the three aspects of the Goddess: maiden, mother, and crone. When the moon is moving from new to full we refer to it as waxing because the light is waxing, or growing fuller. It is traditional to work magic for increase or gain during this moon phase. When the moon is moving from full to dark it is called a waning moon because the light decreases. This is the time to use magic to rid yourself of unwanted influences or to decrease some negative qualities or situations in your life. Throughout this book you will see suggested moon phases for working a particular spell. You can obtain an astrological calendar or almanac to keep track of the moon. You can also consult the weather box in your local newspaper. Most papers list dates for new and full moons.

HEALTH AND BEAUTY

WEIGHT LOSS SPELLS

The first rule of thumb is no shopping in the snack aisle! These spells are intended to reinforce and empower the path you have already chosen to lose weight. The first spell is to be used in conjunction with weight loss plans that use diet and/or physical exercise as a means to slim down. The second is a spell to increase determination and willpower for sticking to any plan and will help you meet your desired ends. It is best to work both of these spells from a full moon to a waning moon, in other words, during the time of decrease. As the crescent grows smaller so will you.

POTATO SPELL

Ingredients

  anise seeds or licorice
  potato

Potatoes are ruled by the moon and endowed with the properties of protection and compassion. Working with them counteracts the tendency to be unkind to yourself or drive yourself too hard in your quest to lose weight. You want to insure that you are not harming your body in the process. Begin by peeling a potato and carving into the surface the number of pounds you want to lose. Continue carving the potato into a human form. Making potato poppets is a very old form of magic known as sympathetic magic. Dating back to Paleolithic times, sympathetic magic is a form of ritual based on the theory that an operation or spell performed on the likeness or image of a real person will produce the same results on the person as well. The doll or poppet becomes you.

Place a lock of your own hair on the head of the potato to create a magical link between you and the doll. Using a knife, mark the potato doll with xs in all the places that you want to slim down. Create a mouth using anise or licorice seeds. (Anise is a natural appetite suppressant. You can also pop some into your own mouth.) Keep the potato doll until you have reached your goal. It is also recommended to work this spell weekly and set a different goal for each week.

HOT STUFF SPELL

Ingredients

> **pepper sauce**
> **celery stalks or carrots**
> **honey**

Take a celery stalk and drizzle a small amount of honey in its center, along with three drops of pepper sauce. As you eat the stalk, visualize yourself being disciplined about food and exercise, and sticking to your general weight loss plan. Also see yourself feeling full and not craving sweets. As the celery becomes smaller and smaller visualize yourself doing the same. Celery is a diuretic and a good diet food. Honey is an appetite suppressant and reduces the urge to eat sugar. Pepper is a commanding spice and can help you control your unhealthy urges. Ruled by the planet Mars, the fiery taste of hot peppers can be used as a mild controlling or compelling formula.

Do not eat more than three stalks a day. Carrots can also be used, as they will increase your drive toward accomplishing tasks. They are ruled by Mars and their orange color represents the color of action.

Lexa Roséan

SPELL TO LOOK MAGNIFICENT

Ingredients

apples
snow peas
avocado
cherries

Remember Snow White and the witch who tried to poison her with an apple? Don't believe all the fairy tales you read. Apples have long been used by witches for love, health, and beauty spells. One old wives' tale mentions eating a half tablespoon of apple cider vinegar a day to retain youthfulness. Norse legend tells how the gods and goddesses eat apples to keep their good looks. Remember the princess and the pea? Another snow job! Peas (especially snow peas) are sacred to Venus, the goddess of beauty. To place a pea pod under your pillow will actually insure that you get your beauty rest. Avocado is another food sacred to Venus. Rich in oils, it is used in countless beauty products to rejuvenate the skin. Cherries promote self-confidence and happiness, keys to feeling beautiful.

Take an apple and cut it in half horizontally. You should find a five-pointed star at its center. This is the witches' magical symbol, representing the perfection of the human form. The top point is the head, the center points are two arms, and the bottom points are two legs. Visualize yourself glowing like a perfect star.

Color also plays a part in this ritual. If you want to look great for romantic reasons, use a red apple. To make someone green with envy or to look good for a job interview, use a green apple. Golden apples are recommended for people in the arts or anyone wanting to make an impression upon the public. Eat half of the apple and give the other half as an offering. Simply place it on your altar or outdoors under a tree.

Now peel the skin off the avocado. The avocado is also known as the alligator pear. Imagine all your "alligator" traits being removed. The alligator lives in dark, swampy areas. Release all the murky and unattractive thoughts you have about yourself, shedding them with the skin of the avocado. Slice the fruit into seven pieces and remove the pit. (Seven is the sacred number of Venus.) Mash the slices into a paste as if you were making guacamole. Use the paste as a face mask. As you cover your face visualize all your blemishes disappearing.

Now take seven peas in the right hand and seven cherries in the left hand. Eat them alternately. The left hand rules the subconscious and unseen world, while the right hand rules the conscious and "seen" world. What you are doing is simultaneously creating beauty both within and without. This ritual should be done at least one to three days before you intend to strut your stuff.

SPELLS FOR LONGEVITY

Ingredients

> **dried apricots**
> **apples**
> **sunflower seeds**
> **pears**
> **olives**
> **beets**

In the foothills of the Himalayan Mountains in northern Pakistan, it is said that 120-year-old men play soccer with young boys. Two of the main staples of their diet are dried apricots and apricot juice. Many people consider apricots to be effective in preventing premature heart attacks, raising vital mineral levels in post-menopausal women, and because of their high level of beta-carotene, they are believed to block the formation of certain cancers.

Everyone knows the old adage, "An apple a day keeps the doctor away." It is said that even smelling apples can make one live longer. Sunflower seeds are sacred to Apollo, the Sun God who bestowed the gifts of healing and prophecy. In Chinese lore the pear tree is said to bear fruit for up to three hundred years. Olive trees are known to live up to three thousand years. The Bible mentions the use of olives and olive oil as a curative and certain medical findings suggest that antioxidants, such as the ones in olives, may help prevent cancer.

Beets are ruled by Saturn or Father Time and people have always eaten them to invoke long and healthy lives. Simply incorporating any or all of these foods into the daily diet can magically lengthen your life span.

"May you live 120 years" is a popular Hebrew blessing. One hundred twenty is also a magical number representing totality and completion. Count out 120 sunflower seeds and eat them at sunrise. Or, offer them to someone you love on their birthday. Wait until the end of the "Happy Birthday" song then add the words "and many more" as you pour the seeds into their hands.

When you eat pears or olives imagine yourself being endowed with the longevity of the trees that bear them. Spread your arms out and plant your feet firmly on the ground. See yourself as the tree and visualize dropping seeds into the earth around you. In this way you can extend the blessing of long life to your offspring.

It is said that rubbing an apple and then eating it can make a wish come true. Dab a bit of olive or apricot oil into your palm. Rub it into the apple and make a wish for long life. Bite into the apple and visualize yourself being healthy in your old age.

Drink beet and apple juice, focusing on the liquid as it moves down your throat and into your stomach. Visualize a vibrant golden-red light filling your aura and every single cell with life energy.

SPELL TO CURE INSOMNIA

Ingredients

> **three slices of turkey**
> **chamomile tea or hot milk**
> **nutmeg and oregano**

Hot milk is an old remedy to bring on sleep. The presence of lactose acts as a sedative; milk, because it is sacred to the Mother Goddess, contains the spiritual power to comfort, soothe, and nurture. Turkey contains tryptophan, an amino acid that causes drowsiness. When you find yourself tossing and turning, head toward the kitchen and make yourself a midnight snack to cure your insomnia. Three slices of turkey and a glass of hot milk or chamomile tea should do the trick. Chamomile tea soothes nerves and can also bring on sleep.

Nutmeg is a spice originally brought to Europe from Indonesia. Its medicinal and magical properties were believed to be similar to those of opiates or peyote. The Native American shamans would eat peyote before embarking on vision quests. The drug caused nausea and then hallucinations. It also created a sense of well-being and put them in a dream- or trancelike state. Eating too much nutmeg will also induce vomiting. Just sprinkle a small amount on your hot milk. After drinking, place your head on a pillow and allow the subtle influence of the nutmeg to lead you into the sacred dream world. Succumb to the magical images that dance behind your eyelids.

If nightmares are the cause of your sleeplessness, place a whole nutmeg and a sprinkling of oregano under your pillow to insure peaceful dreams. The etymology of the word *oregano* means mountain brightness or joy. It is a delicate seasoning sacred to Mercury and Neptune, bestowing protection and inducing a calm, meditative, dreamy state. The combination of nutmeg and oregano will allow even the most resistant mind to let go and sail off with Wynken, Blynken, and Nod.

SPELL TO QUIT SMOKING OR TO BREAK A BAD HABIT

Ingredients

dental floss
cloves
coffee beans
pepper

Cloves are used for luck and influence. Coffee is used to strengthen a commitment to work. The combination of the two creates a mild compelling formula. If you add a pinch of pepper, you will have a strong commanding formula. Decide whether you need a slap on the wrist or a hammer over the head to end your nasty habit. Take an empty jar and fill it halfway with coffee beans. Add three cloves (and perhaps a pinch of pepper). Shake the bottle anytime you feel the urge to smoke. You can also add a few cigarette butts to the jar (or a pinch of whatever substance you are abusing). Keep the jar near you and shake it whenever you feel your willpower slipping away.

Another method is to use a binding spell. Binding is an ancient method of magic used by witches to stop the influence or power of something. It also can be used to gain control over a person, substance or situation. Witches use cords to bind, but we will use dental floss as a substitute because its very nature involves the removal of harmful bacteria from our mouths. We will imbue dental floss with the power to remove cigarettes from our mouths, in the same way that it literally removes plaque from between our teeth.

Dental floss has other magical components that will make the spell more potent. Choose a *waxed* floss with *mint* flavoring. Wax is a sacred tool for witches, used to fashion candles and form magical seals. Sealing something with wax will always strengthen a spell. Mint is an herb used for purification, healing, and to influence our thoughts. These properties are all conducive to the intent of this spell. Simply take nine feet of dental floss. (The number nine represents completion and can be used to bring an end to something.) Wrap it carefully around a cigarette and tie nine knots. As you tie each knot, repeat this chant:

> I bind you with the circle of nine.
> Now the power over you is mine.
> If you should tempt me, I will attack
> and mercilessly break your back.

On the last verse, pull the floss tightly and break the cigarette in two.

Visualize yourself breaking the habit.

SPELL TO RELIEVE STRESS

Ingredients

>   **ginger**
>   **sugar**
>   **sea salt**
>   **lemon**
>   **cardamom**
>   **chamomile tea**

There are several ways to utilize this spell. Draw a bath and add three chamomile tea bags, a whole ginger root, three fistfuls of sugar, three fistfuls of salt, a teaspoon of ground cardamom seeds, and the juice of a whole lemon. Relax and soak in the tub. Or, brew a cup of chamomile tea and add a pinch each of salt, cardamom, and ginger. Then add lemon and sugar to taste. Drink the tea before, during, or after any stressful situation.

The third preparation is to be used as a massage therapy for muscle tension in the body. Brew a tea as described above, but do not add the salt. Fill an empty mayonnaise jar with sea salt and then pour the tea over it. Shake well. You now have a salt rub to use on specific areas of your body that hold tension and stress. Salt is a purifier. It removes negativity from the body. The use of salts in baths and massage dates back to ancient Egypt. Sugar is to remind you of the sweetness of life. Lemon cleanses and refreshes. Cardamom relaxes. Ginger stimulates circulation and has long been used in the Orient for healing. Cardamom and ginger are often used in love rituals as well. The element of self-love is crucial to maintaining a stress-free and healthy body.

SPELL TO WARD OFF A WINTER COLD OR FLU

Ingredients

   any pine cleaner
   lemons or lemon oil
   apple cider vinegar

Many household cleaning products have magical purposes as well as practical ones. It is important to think about these added benefits while you use them. Of course the selling point is that this product will make your home spick-and-span, clean and bright like the sun. The spiritual point is that the sun also brings warmth and is the orb of health and well-being. So by using these products you are not only cleaning your home on a physical level but on the spiritual plane as well.

Try to incorporate the magical symbols (names or logos) of the products you buy into this ritual. Symbols are the wheels of magic. Intent is magic's engine, its driving force. Every product you handle holds power in its name, origin, or logo. Your purpose determines where and how that power will be utilized. Colors are significant as well. A yellow product invokes the attributes of the sun mentioned above. Green is the color of abundance and also of healing, while blue is the color of peace and protection.

The most common disinfectants are pine and lemon. Pine wards off illness in a home. Lemon is an excellent cleanser and removes negative energy. Apple cider vinegar can be used as an internal or external purge and strengthens the immune system. Make a floor wash with a tablespoon of apple cider vinegar and a capful each of pine cleaner and lemon oil. Wash down the rooms in your house. You can also clean the tub with a pine cleaner and then take a bath, adding the juice of two lemons and two tablespoons of apple cider vinegar to a tub of bathwater. Also drinking water with a teaspoon of apple cider vinegar or a squeeze of lemon and honey can help ward off a cold.

OBSTACLES AND ENEMIES

THE OBSTACLE REMOVER SPELL

Ingredients

> **powdered drain opener**
> **plastic wrap**
> **eggshells**
> **black magic marker**
> **empty mayonnaise jar**

Fill a mayonnaise jar with powdered drain opener. Cut a small slit in the top of the jar lid so you can shake the powder out to spell words, kind of like decorating a cake. Write out your obstacle with powdered drain opener on a cutting board. (Cover the board with plastic wrap to protect it.) Then shake the contents down the sink. Visualize pipes being unclogged—in the same way your obstacle will be removed.

The same spell can be done in a different fashion if you have a garbage disposal in your kitchen sink. In this case write the obstacle on the inside of a white eggshell using black ink. The color black is used to cut or blast through negativity. In fact, black and white are the most powerful colors used in witchcraft to dispel evil, or to clear one's path and free it of obstacles. There is a very sacred substance used in voodoo rituals called cascarilla. Made out of powdered eggshells, cascarilla is used to ward off adversity and is offered to the gods in exchange for them clearing your path. Drop the eggshell down the sink and turn on the garbage disposal. Let it rip. Visualize your obstacle being pulverized to smithereens. Pray to the divine ones that your path in life be free of roadblocks.

EGGSTERMINATOR SPELLS

Ingredients

  eggs

> Humpty Dumpty sat on a wall,
> Humpty Dumpty had a great fall.
> All the king's horses and all the king's men
> Couldn't put Humpty together again.

Not true. The regenerative powers of eggs are remarkable. The egg is symbolic of the life force. The most sacred symbol of the Goddess and creation, it carries great healing powers. Eggs are great stress relievers. They can absorb negative and excess emotional energy. As a matter of fact, eggs are such excellent absorbers I never recommend ingesting one without salting it first. Salt is a purifier. If you salt the egg you can insure you will not ingest any negative energy the egg may have absorbed. In general it is never advisable to eat foods you have worked with to remove blocks or obstacles. Otherwise those blocks will just reenter the body.

SPELL TO BANISH NEGATIVITY

An excellent spell is simply to take a hot bath and delicately place an egg in the tub with you. Be careful not to break it. Just let it gently float around in the tub with you and banish your negative energy, whether it be sorrow, pain, fear, anger, stress, worry, etc. When you exit the tub, allow all the water to drain before removing the egg.

SPELL TO REMOVE ASTRAL CHORDS FROM EX-LOVERS

In my many years of counseling I have found this spell quite useful. When a relationship has ended, the emotional residue must be cleared away. Otherwise people have trouble moving on to their next relationship even though they've been divorced or separated for years. The dregs of the relationship continue to cause adverse effects. Example: getting butterflies in the stomach when you unexpectedly run into your ex. Once you initiate sexual contact with another person, you form astral chords with them. Invisible to the naked eye, these chords will remain in place unless they are consciously removed. Their influence may vary from mild discomfort, occasional dreams, or sensing when the person will call, to full-blown anxiety attacks causing insomnia, melancholia, and acute awareness of any sexual activity that person initiates with another. Wow! When you feel it is time to let go, proceed as follows.

Stand naked in your room. Take a whole raw egg that has reached room temperature and place it carefully at the crown of your head. Using both hands move the egg counterclockwise down and around the whole body. When you reach your feet, rub the soles with the egg. As you slowly move the egg across your body, visualize your ex-lover. Allow whatever thoughts, feelings, memories, and emotions that surface to be explored. Do not try to control this process. If you feel like laughing, laugh, if you feel like crying, cry. Do not censor your emotions. However, if you feel angry, if you feel like breaking the egg, don't. Be very careful. At no time must the egg break until the end of the ritual.

To dispose of the egg, throw it down the toilet (if you have good plumbing). If it breaks, fine. If not, that's also fine. The second method of disposal is to throw the egg in a paper bag, crumble up the bag, and take it outside of your house. Follow up this ritual with a nice salt bath.

Note: This spell will not physically remove these people from your life. That is not its purpose. The intent is to bring you back to your center, to create a neutral space emotionally so they can no longer "push your buttons."

For those inclined towards promiscuity, I recommend keeping a few dozen eggs on hand.

THE EGGCELLENT TREASURE HUNT SPELL

Do you feel negative energy in your home? Here's how to remove it. Hide seven eggs in the areas where you feel the negativity. (Make sure to place them out of the line of traffic.) Leave them there for one full moon cycle, then collect the eggs and dispose of them outside the house. All negative energy will be removed.

Note: If you are absentminded or suffer from short-term memory loss, please jot down all the places you have stashed the eggs. Should you forget to do this or lose the paper you recorded it on, don't worry! By the time four full moon cycles have passed, the smell of rotten eggs will lead you to any forgotten hiding places.

SPRING TREAT SPELL

Ingredients

  one dozen eggs
  food coloring

Spring is the season of renewal. It is interesting to note that the egg plays an important role in many spring holidays. The Jewish Passover uses the egg as one of the five symbols on the seder plate. Colored Easter eggs are a traditional symbol at Easter. The custom actually stems from the old pagan worship of the goddesses Eostre or Astarte. Modern witches celebrating the spring equinox use red-colored eggs on their altars to symbolize the lifeblood of the Mother Goddess.

There is a secular egg ritual practiced on the spring equinox (March 21–23) as well. Once a year for about fifteen minutes during the equinox hour, the magnetic polarities between the Earth, sun, and moon make it possible to stand an egg on its end. Try this feat at any other point in the year and I assure you it will not work. The egg will simply roll over on its side. Although there are scientific explanations for this amazing phenomenon, witches tend to view it as a confirmation from the Goddess of her continued renewal. Just as the rainbow is a symbol in the Old Testament of the end of the deluge, the egg standing on end foretells the end of winter and promises the rebirth of spring.

Here is a spring ritual to promote renewal. It can be used by anyone of any faith. Take some hard-boiled eggs and dye them with food coloring. The color of the eggs is very symbolic. Red for love or honoring the Goddess, green for money or fertility, blue for peace and protection, yellow for happiness and health, orange for success and creativity, purple for strength and power. Plant wishes within them for yourself and your loved ones. This can be done by carefully writing the wishes on the outer shell or by holding the egg in both hands and mentally projecting your wishes into it. Next, bury the eggs outdoors. This provides a spiritual incubation period for the wishes. They will be charged with the positive and reproductive powers of the Earth. Have your loved ones search for the eggs. When they are discovered the wishes will manifest themselves and be born of the eggs as they are opened. As each egg is eaten, those qualities or wishes will be planted and begin to grow within the individual.

Teutonic tribes living about one hundred years before the birth of Christ had a custom of burying eggs to infuse the Earth with life-giving forces. If you would like to use your magical energy to heal the planet, bury some eggs and do not dig them up. Let the Earth keep their good wishes. The color red is appropriate to honor the Earth Mother, while green can be used for "keeping the earth green." Your wish can be for the fertility of the rain forests or simply be directed toward your own garden. Blue would be used to protect the oceans and to encourage world peace.

SPELL TO REMOVE UNWANTED GUESTS

Ingredients

  vinegar
  red pepper
  laundry detergent
  stain remover

Has someone worn out his or her welcome? Launder his or her clothes separately from the rest of the family. Add nine pinches of pepper and a teaspoon of vinegar along with a cup of detergent. Pepper and vinegar are both irritants and together they are used in magic spells to turn someone away. In Southern lore pepper and vinegar were sprinkled across a doorstep to keep people from entering. Sprinkle stain remover into the washer in a counterclockwise or banishing circle. As you do this shout three times: *"(Name here) out!"* Within two weeks of wearing these clothes that person should leave. If not, repeat the spell sans soap. The person will either leave or ask you to stop washing his or her laundry.

SPELL TO GET SOMEONE OUT OF YOUR LIFE

Ingredients

   red cayenne pepper
   sea salt
   kitchen matches
   1 small candle
   nine pennies

Empty out two-thirds of the pepper from its bottle. Fill the b a third full of sea salt. Break the heads off the matches and u heads to fill the jar almost to the top. Match heads contain s magical element used by witches to scatter negative forces. Sea salt is for cleansing and cayenne pepper makes things uncomfortable for people who try to harm you. Write the name of the person you want away from you on a small piece of paper. (If you have a signature, even better). Insert the paper into the jar. Close the lid tightly. For nine days in a row beginning ten days before the new moon, shake the bottle as many times a day as you feel inclined to do so. Visualize this person moving away from you. On the ninth day rub the lid of the jar with the wax of a candle. (Any color is suitable but black is best.) Take the jar to the closest river and throw it in. Throw nine pennies over your shoulder and don't look back.

Note: Because of the Law of Return, (Witches believe that whatever magic you do, good or evil, it will return to you threefold) it is advisable to make your visualizations positive. For example, say you are working this spell on an ex-lover who has been stalking you. Instead of picturing him or her getting hit by a truck, try to imagine this person getting a fabulous new job three thousand miles away and, once there, meeting the love of his or her life.

CLEANSING BATH SPELL

Ingredients

    bay leaves
    1 lemon

flour
sea salt

This recipe is used to unhex or unvex yourself. It does not matter whether the negative energy is coming from an internal or an external source. It can also be used to remove any sort of obstacle from your path. Simply add nine bay leaves, the juice of a whole lemon, three fistfuls of sea salt, and a sprinkling of flour to a full tub. Three and nine are numbers of completion. You want to make sure the cleansing is thorough.

Bay is ruled by the sun and is used for protection and purification. In ancient Greece, the priestesses of the Delphic oracle would chew bay leaves to open their psychic channels. As you sit in the tub, chew on a bay leaf and meditate on the source of your problems. Answers or messages should come. In Rome, bay was used to ward off evil and is still burned or scattered in modern exorcism rites. During the Middle Ages, bay was used to protect against witchcraft. You can carry three leaves in your pocket if you feel someone is actively working magic against you. Flour is used for purification and stabilization. The combination of lemon and salt is used to drive away evil. You must sit in the tub for at least ten minutes and immerse yourself completely three times. Do not towel off but allow yourself to air-dry.

SPELL TO WARD OFF THE BOOGEYMAN

Ingredients

spring water
sea salt

This is one of the simplest and most effective spells for warding off any negative night energy, and is quite effective for banishing nightmares. It was given to me by my high priestess, Lady Miw. Many children and even adults are afraid of the dark. It's spooky! Night is the traditional time when spirits and demons rule. During the Middle Ages people never went out at night for fear of catching their death.

To ward off evil spirits or bad dreams, place a bowl of fresh spring water on the bedstand. Slowly add a pinch of sea salt and say, "Evil spirits touch not me nor mine. Thy power I drain into this brine." You must use three pinches of salt in total and repeat the verse as you add each pinch. In the morning empty the bowl down the toilet or sink. Repeat as often as necessary.

SPELL TO EXORCISE DEMONS

Ingredients

1 new broom or a vacuum cleaner
one white Sabbath candle
kosher or sea salt
spring water
leeks

FROM A DWELLING

Sweep your entire house counterclockwise with a new broom. Then open the door and make a broad and forceful sweep out the door. Shout: "I banish you. I banish you. I banish you. Be gone!" Visualize the negative forces departing. Of course, if you have a vacuum cleaner just vacuum the whole house against the clock, then dispose of the vacuum bag outside your home using the same words and visualization.

Take a sprig from the heart of a leek and then cut it in half. Slice a small slit in the center of one half. Slip the other half through it to form a cross. Add it to a bowl of spring water with three pinches of sea salt. Walk clockwise around the whole house sprinkling the water. The salt water is used for general cleansing. Leeks will strengthen and protect the auric field of your home. In medieval times leeks were believed to protect against ghosts, demons, and thunder. So strong was this belief that at one point, Charlemagne, the founder of the Holy Roman Empire, ordered leeks to be planted on every rooftop. Fashioning the leek in the shape of a cross symbolizes the four corners of your home. You are sealing off all four directions to prevent the demon from reentering. Walk clockwise again with the lighted candle lighting all the dark corners of your home. Visualize a vibrant circle of protective white light and say, "I do purify and cleanse this space, removing all negativity and invoking good herein." To insure the success of this ritual, you may save the leek cross. Let it dry and then permanently hang it above your front door.

If you have been experiencing poltergeist activity, hang bay leaves above all the doors and windows. They have been used since the Middle Ages to ward off ghosts and lightning.

FROM A PERSON

Lightly tap the possessed with a new broom. Begin at the crown of the head and spiral counterclockwise down to the feet. Shave or cut off the bottom layer of the broom bristles and burn them. As you tap the subject shout, "Out!" "Leave now!" or "Go away!" When you burn the bristles say, "I banish you. I banish you. I banish you. Be gone." Fix the exorcised person a bowl of steamed and salted leeks. Ingesting leeks strengthens the physical and the astral body. It is said that those of weak mental, physical, or spiritual states are most easily possessed. Let them eat in front of a burning white candle. Mentally draw a protective circle of white light around the subject and have them quietly recite a traditional prayer from their own faith or a simple prayer in their own words.

Warning: Do not attempt to vacuum an evil spirit out of a human subject.

SPELL TO CONFUSE AN ENEMY OR COMPETITOR

Ingredients

> **blueberries**
> **double-ply tissues**
> **cotton swab**

The earliest growth and use of cotton was in India. After the conquests of Alexander it was brought to Greece and later on to the Americas. The first cotton picked in a field would usually be prayed over to yield a good crop. In American slave lore cotton was used in spells for luck, love, communication, and protection. It was also believed to drive away evil, cause abortions, and thwart an enemy's plans. Blueberries are a traditional magical ingredient for protection and warding off or confusing an enemy.

Take a handful of blueberries and wrap them in double-ply tissues. Smash them with your fist and grind them to a pulp. Open up the tissues and, using a cotton swab, paint the name of your enemy or competitor backwards on another tissue with the blueberry pulp. Throw the tissue up in the air and blow it this way and that. In the same way your enemy will be blown about and be unable to follow your trail.

THE "FREEZE-YOUR-ENEMY" SPELL

This spell is not dangerous unless it is done with malicious intent. If you use it to stop another's harmful actions toward you, the spell is positive. If you visualize harm coming to another, the spell is negative. I leave it to your discretion.

Ingredients

> 1 plastic ice cube tray
> 1 piece of paper
> water
> sugar or honey (optional)

Do you have twelve enemies you want to keep at bay? Buy a blue ice tray. Write the names of your foes on small pieces of paper and lay one in each cubicle. If you have a signature it is even more effective. Then fill the tray with water and place it in the freezer. This will prevent the person from taking any negative action against you. If you want to sweeten someone up (perhaps a boss or a mother-in-law), add a drop of honey or a pinch of sugar to the water.

For the suburban version of this spell, simply place the middle finger of your right hand on the automatic ice-dispenser button of your freezer. Chant your enemy's name seven times as the ice pours out into the tray. Do not use this ice in your beverages. Collect it in a Tupperware container, let it melt down, and then refreeze it in the Tupperware container until such time as you feel it is no longer needed.

THE "YOU DIRTY RAT" SPELL

Ingredients

> **one or more house cats**
> **cat litter box**
> **kitty litter**

According to my friend Cindy Gardner, who knows more household hints than Heloise, you don't really need a cat to get rid of mice and rats. Simply borrow a few scoops of well-used cat litter from a neighbor and sprinkle it around the house. The smell alone will make those dirty rats scat immediately! (Never underestimate the power of positive stinking.)

Place a picture of your most hated enemy in a clean cat litter tray. Cover it with fresh litter and let the cats at it. Replace the picture after each time you clean the box. The effects of this spell are very unpleasant, especially to the olfactory senses. Your foe will sense the smell of cat urine or feces every time they try to cross your path without knowing quite where it's coming from. Although not particularly harmful, this spell can be quite mischievous and produce mildly neurotic behavior in your opponent. For instance, those countless hours previously spent planning your demise will now be used up obsessively checking the bottoms of shoes, bathing, shopping for new deodorants, and cleaning rugs, searching for the source of the odor.

Warning: In severe cases nausea and loss of appetite may occur, eventually resulting in death by starvation.

Note: This spell is considered black magic unless the cats are albinos.

SPELL TO LET GO OF UNPLEASANT FEELINGS

Ingredients

  one onion

I offer this spell as an option to all the enemy spells. It is quite effective and spiritually regenerative. Simply stand alone in a dimly lit room, preferably when the moon is dark, and peel an onion. Onions are ruled by Mars and are used to draw anger or negativity to the surface. Onions open the heart chakra, which is why we cry when we cut them. In esoteric philosophy, anger is the layer covering pain or sorrow, and sorrow is the key to wisdom and understanding. In many situations it is our ego that has been damaged and that prompts us to seek revenge. The onion's spiritual vibration compels us to peel away the ego and helps us to see things through another's eyes. Onions bring clarity and cleanse the emotional body. As each layer is removed from the onion, feel the layers of emotional baggage being removed from your heart. Peel away hatred, envy, jealousy, and pain. This spell is very effective with love relationships that have turned bitter or hateful. After performing this spell, you should no longer possess the desire to "get even." Follow up this ritual with a warm bath, adding to the tub three fistfuls of kosher or sea salt, a tablespoon of rose water or sweet condensed milk, and a pinch of oat bran. These ingredients will maintain a positive and healing vibration in your heart center. As you soak in the tub meditate upon what you have learned from the situation by not "getting even."

Sex, Love, Relationships, Marriage

A LOVE SPELL FOR A VALENTINE

Ingredients

> **2 fig cookies or raw figs**
> **vanilla extract**
> **cookie cutter**

Figs were sacred to the love goddesses Aphrodite, Venus, Ishtar, and Astarte. Some say the fruit that Eve used to tempt Adam was not an apple but a fig. In ancient Babylonia under the rule of the Goddess, it was considered a sacred fruit that represented the female genitals. To make the sign of the fig (make a fist and place the thumb between the pointer and middle fingers) was considered a sign of protection and blessing because it invoked the Great Mother. In fact, the fig hand was so powerful that medieval church fathers called it obscene. As men built churches upon the ruins of ancient goddess shrines all over Europe, the fig hand became a derogatory gesture similar to raising the middle finger at someone. Thus men are particularly vulnerable to the magic of figs.

Take two fig cookies or raw figs and cut them into perfect hearts. Carve the initials of you and your loved one in the center of the heart. Pick up a bottle of pure vanilla extract. Vanilla is said to stimulate the appetite of love. Yum. Dab some vanilla extract on your thumb and trace the outer edges of the hearts, saturating the fig filling with essence of vanilla. Then feed the hearts to each other with your hands crossing over each other as you do so. This spell works best when done after a romantic dinner. The dessert figs should put you in the mood for lovemaking. However, these little hearts can also be the perfect snack to shove in your husband's mouth during *Monday Night Football.* You may need to feed him half a dozen but you should be able to obtain the desired effect before halftime.

To win someone's heart, do not carve any initials on the surface but trace your own initials delicately in the heart's center with vanilla extract. Let it dry and become invisible, then feed it to your intended. To keep a lover faithful grind up two coriander seeds and rub them along the outer lining of the fig along with the vanilla extract. This last spell may need to be repeated every full moon.

YAM LOVE SPELL

Ingredients

> male yam (yang)
> female yam (yin)

Male yams are long in shape, while females are round. Whether you are a male or female, you can eat male yams to increase your yang energy or female yams to increase your yin energy. Sometimes women need to be more outgoing, therefore they should eat yang yams. Sometimes men need to get in touch with their softer side and should eat yin yams. Again, a man may need more male energy or a woman may need more feminine energy. The best state of being is a perfect balance of yin and yang within each individual. To make a relationship more balanced and complete, eat both types with your partner. Yams can also be eaten for fertility.

MARRIAGE SPELLS

Ingredients

> 1 orange
> spring water (can substitute maple syrup)
> rose water
> nutmeg

rice
1 whole coconut

Oranges have been used for centuries to attract spiritual and sexual love. It is said that neroli oil (the blossom of the orange) was one of the rare spices the Queen of Sheba used to seduce King Solomon. According to Greek myth, Jupiter gave Juno an orange as a wedding gift and ever since, the orange blossom has been a traditional bridal flower. Rose water attracts love and friendship. Spring water represents purity.

Maple syrup is ruled by Jupiter and draws love and prosperity. There are various tales told about how maple came to the native North Americans. Some say it was a gift from the gods. Others claim it was discovered accidentally by a squaw too lazy to collect water from the spring to cook her stew. Instead she tapped a nearby tree and it leaked maple sap. The woman ran off in horror when her stew turned into sticky goo. But her husband loved the meal and searched far and wide for her. When he found her, he brought her home and treated her like a queen for the rest of her days. (Royalty is *not* an equal substitute for purity. Use the spring water if marrying a virgin is a top priority. Otherwise purity is better suited to people seeking a life of celibacy and fasting.) Nutmeg brings trust, understanding, and communication. The custom of throwing rice at newlyweds originated in China. It bestowed upon the couple luck and fertility, while in some ancient cultures eating rice from a common bowl symbolized the binding of the souls of the marriage partners. Coconuts are sacred to the moon goddess, ruler of the home. They are used for love and purification rituals.

Take a whole coconut. Drain the milk (keep it) and then split the coconut in half. Use the larger half of the coconut as a mixing bowl. In African-Cuban magic the coconut half is considered a sacred vessel. Pour some of the milk back in and mix with rose water and spring water (or a thimbleful of maple syrup). Squeeze in the juice of an orange. Stir clockwise seven times with the thumb of your left hand. Sprinkle a pinch of nutmeg over the top, all the while visualizing your loved one proposing to you. If you don't have anyone specific in mind, visualize someone coming into your life with the qualities you are looking for. When you feel that the visualization is very strong, throw three fistfuls of rice into the brew, chanting "I do, I do, I do." Cover the coconut with its other half and place under your bed. Sprinkle the mixture around your bed in the morning while calling out the name of your intended. Repeat for seven nights. Repeat this every new moon until you have obtained your desire.

The Cabala is the mystic theosophy of Judaism. It is a compilation of magical lore handed down through the ages and includes esoteric interpretations of the Bible based on the belief that every word and letter has an occult meaning. An old Cabalistic legend says that if you peel an orange in one whole piece and place the peel under your pillow on the full moon, you will dream of the one you are to marry.

SPELLS FOR DOMESTIC BLISS

Ingredients

> **cabbage or cole slaw**
> **lima or kidney beans**

Cabbage blesses a marriage. It should be eaten once a month, preferably on the new moon, to strengthen the union, reawaken couples to their vows, and avoid any domestic problems. Ruled by the moon, cabbage can either increase or decrease a situation. If you would like to enhance certain aspects of your relationship, serve cabbage on a waxing moon. Do not cut it, but boil it whole and allow the leaves to soften and then gently seperate. Or, cook them into a thick soup. Soups are also ruled by the moon and are said to protect families. If you would like to end a particular problem in your relationship, cut the cabbage up during a waning moon. Visualize the negative situation decreasing or you and your mate "cutting through" the obstacles as you shred the cabbage. Prepare a slaw, since tossing is a good magical action to eliminate grievances. If the problems seem overwhelming, "toss" them up to the gods and pray for solutions. If money is the source of the problem, eat green cabbage. In ancient Rome, green cabbage was cooked with a silver coin and eaten to increase prosperity.

If you have already run into serious domestic problems and are considering divorce, serve lima or kidney beans. They can alleviate tension and end arguments and can help couples to constructively work out their problems. According to Indian mythology, all foods have Ayur/Vedic (medicinal/spiritual) properties. Lima and kidney beans have both a hard and a soft nature. They are used to balance the male and female principles and to strengthen intimacy. It is said that when love is blocked, fear takes over. The beans help to soften the fear and reopen the channels for love. The shape of these beans is highly significant. According to the Tao, an ancient Chinese philosophy, the kidneys are called "the root of life." All sexual energy stems from the kidneys. The negative emotions associated with the organ are fear and stress, while the positive emotion is gentleness. Lima and kidney beans share the spiritual properties of the kidney because of their likeness in shape. Eat these beans to get to the root of your problems.

It is also believed that the kidneys determine the length of your life. Using your eye, try to scoop an equal portion of beans on two separate plates. Count the number of beans that fall upon your plate. Compare them to the number of beans on your spouse's plate. If they are equal you will remain together till death do you part. If one or the other has more beans, that will be the number of months you have left to solve your problems in a constructive way so that you may remain together.

CLEOPATRA SALAD SPELL

Ingredients

> **romaine lettuce**
> **asparagus**
> **tomatoes**
> **snow peas**
> **hearts of palm**
> **pitted black olives**
> **1 garlic clove**
> **radishes**
> **orange flower water or rose water or a tangerine**

This salad is consumed to make yourself more attractive, to invoke beauty, or to bewitch someone. Lettuce was sacred to the Egyptian phallic god Min. Asparagus is sacred to the sexy Roman god Mars. Tomatoes and snow peas are sacred to voluptuous Venus. Hearts of palm, garlic, and black olives are aphrodisiacs. Red radishes create lust but can also protect you from unwanted sexual advances.

As you wash all the vegetables visualize your sexual aura increasing. As you chop the vegetables visualize the sharpness and definition of your beauty. See yourself captivating the man or woman you desire. Lastly, place the ingredients in a wooden bowl you have rubbed with garlic. Then sprinkle with orange flower or rose water, or juice squeezed from a tangerine. All are used to attract love. If you consume the salad, it will increase your animal magnetism and drawing power. If eaten by another while in your presence, it will make you irresistible to them. Look out, Caesar. The Queen of the Nile has a salad to beguile.

APPLE LOVE SPELL

Ingredients

  1 apple
  a paring knife

"He loves me. She loves me not. She loves me. He loves me not." Don't pluck the daisy petals. Here's an easier way to find out how he or she feels. Cut an apple in half. Offer half to your desired. If he or she accepts the apple and eats it, he or she will be yours.

Another ancient apple love spell can determine the initial (first or last) of your true love. Simply twist the stem of an apple. On each rotation call out a letter of the alphabet. Begin with *A*. The letter you call as the stem parts from the apple will be the initial of your true love.

SPELL FOR ENDING A RELATIONSHIP

Ingredients

   eggplant

Eggplants are sacred to the Yoruban goddess Oya, the goddess of cemeteries and death. In general, because of their dark purple color, eggplants are sacred to all crone goddesses and can be used to invoke endings. Simply carve the initials of the two parties involved on opposite ends of the eggplant. Then, using a sharp knife, cut the eggplant in half. Cook and eat your own half and serve the remaining to the person you are leaving. This spell is intended to be used as a closure ritual. Both parties must participate of their own free will. It cannot be used to break up another couple. (For spells of that nature consult the Fidelity and Infidelity chapter.)

SPELL TO PREVENT SEXUAL HARASSMENT

Ingredients

   mothballs
   cedar chips
   sage

Are you being sexually harassed at the office? Camphor gets rid of unwanted passions. Buy a pack of camphor mothballs and hide them around the workplace. This should protect you from unsolicited advances. Camphor is ruled by the moon. It is important to understand that in Wicca, the religion of witchcraft, the moon is worshiped as a triple goddess. The Maiden, her virginal aspect, is symbolized by the color white and manifests as the new moon; the Mother, her fertile and sexual aspect, is symbolized by the color red and manifests as the full moon; and finally the Crone, her wise woman aspect, is symbolized by the color black and manifests as the dark moon. Camphor is sacred to both the Maiden and the Crone because it is white, but turns black when burned. The period between the dark and new moon honors both the warrior and wise aspects of the feminine principle. It represents a combination of the prepubescent and menopausal phases of womanhood, aspects that for the most part remain unexplored and unappreciated in our modern society. Using camphor will enhance these aspects in a woman and take the focus off her sexuality.

If it is unsafe or unwise for you to place things around the office, simply stand between two burning candles, one white and one black, while gently holding a camphor ball in your cupped hands. Meditate or visualize upon how you wish to be treated in the workplace. After ten or fifteen minutes, put the camphor down and slowly move your hands down your body to strengthen your auric field. Start above your head, and keep your hands about an inch and a half away from your body. Move down and when you reach your feet, lift them up one at a time and pass your hands beneath them. This spell is unusually effective for women who enjoy dressing stylishly or "provocatively" but do not enjoy comments from men in the street or at work.

Cedar chips and sage can also be used to end or prevent sexual harassment. This method will work for both men and women. You can locate sage in the spice section of the supermarket. Sometimes you will find fresh sage in the produce section. (Fresh ingredients are always preferred.) Cedar chips are usually found in the same section as camphor mothballs. You may also find a cat litter product made of natural cedar chips. Sage and cedar can be carried in your pocket or sprinkled around the workplace, but are most effective when smudged (burned) in front of a person or in a space. Sage and cedar are sacred in the Native American tradition and are used for purification. Burned together they can cleanse a room of negative or unwholesome energy. If the herbs are sufficiently dry they should be easily ignited. Place them in a small, nonflammable dish or burner and light. Blow gently until the flame is extinguished, but let the herbs continue to smoke. Pass the dish around yourself from head to toe, or walk clockwise around an area. You should notice a difference in the way people treat you or the way they behave in that space once you have smudged it.

FIDELITY AND INFIDELITY

GUESS WHO'S STAYING HOME FOR DINNER SPELL

Ingredients

2 baby lamb chops
rosemary and sage (preferably fresh)
1 head of cauliflower
olive oil

> Mary had a little lamb,
> Its fleece was white as snow,
> And everywhere that Mary went,
> The lamb was sure to go.

Get the picture? Rosemary insures a woman's dominance in the home. It also increases memory and gives longevity to a marriage.

Sage is used to insure fidelity. Cauliflower is brain food and very protective. It is governed by the moon. The moon goddess is the protectress of the household and all affairs of marriage, home, and children. Olive oil, especially Italian, is the lubricant of lovers.

Take seven pinches of rosemary and three pinches of sage. Grind in a mortar and pestle while visualizing your own little lamb becoming compliant. Add two tablespoons of olive oil and season the chops by delicately spreading the mixture over them. Place the meat three to six inches away from the broiler. Grill three to five minutes on each side. Turn over with tongs at halftime. Don't overcook the lamb. Its juices must still be running—you don't want to dry up the well of passion in your relationship. Serve in a bed of steamed cauliflower to keep your mate faithful. Prepare this meal before your birthday or anniversary to jog his or her memory. To increase your lover's desire for you or to cure impotency add two cloves of garlic to the seasoning.

THE HAPPY HOME BREAKER

Ingredients

watermelon
cantaloupe
red food coloring
spring water

Interested in breaking the seventh commandment? Watermelon can be used to seduce married men. Eat a watermelon while thinking lustful and seductive thoughts. Spit the seeds into a gutted canta- loupe half filled with sugar, water, and red food coloring. Let this mixture sit for seven days underneath your bed. On the full moon, place the seeds in his path and he is sure to slip out of his marriage bonds.

HAPPY HOME BREAKER 2

Ingredients

> 3 gingerbread men or women cookies
> black peppercorns
> horseradish
> honey

Ginger is a hot spice ruled by Mars and used in China for healing and sexual prowess. In Western magic, it is considered a fast-luck herb and is used to speed up a love attraction or money spell. Take two gingerbread men or women cookies. One will symbolize the per- son you desire. The other will symbolize his or her present spouse. Place the cookies next to each other, with the cookie representing the spouse turned upside down. Place a row of peppercorns in between the two. Let the arrangement sit for two days. On the third day, move your intended further away from the spouse and make a second line between them using shavings from a raw horseradish. (If you must, use the bottled kind.) The pepper and horseradish are used to create arguments and separation. On the fourth day place a cookie representing yourself on the other side of your intended. For the next three days slowly move the middle cookie further and further away from the spouse and closer to you. On the seventh day, you and your desired should be touching. Pour a generous amount of honey over both cookies to insure that the two of you stick together.

Note: You can also add a fourth cookie to insure the spouse finds a new mate. Also, you can undo this spell by simply reversing it if you find out you've ultimately bitten off more than you can chew.

SPELLS TO WARD OFF THE HAPPY HOME BREAKER

Ingredients

> **cumin**
> **rhubarb pie**
> **chocolate**
> **cracked peppercorns**
> **black control-top panty hose**

Sprinkle cumin on your spouse's pillow and in his or her shoes to give him or her strength in the face of temptation and to protect your spouse from being bewitched.

Serving your spouse rhubarb pie on a full moon will ward off infidelity.

Scientists (as well as witches!) say that chocolate produces the same effects on the brain as falling in love does. Pepper, with its harsh flavor, closes up the esophagus. It is like running into a stop sign or pulling the emergency brake. The spice is sacred to Mars in his war aspect and can be used to control, hinder, stop, or confuse people. To mix one part chocolate to five parts pepper is like a slap across the face, bringing someone to his or her senses. To mix one part chocolate to nine parts pepper is akin to receiving a high-voltage shock as punishment for feeling something forbidden. Of course, to proportion them the other way round can mildly control someone, causing him or her to give in to your sexual whims. Pay attention to your measurements with this spell. If someone is out to break up your home, you want to give the happy home breaker a searing message to stay away.

Heat up the chocolate on the stove. Slowly and deliberately add your cracked peppercorns, and bring it to a boil. Pour the mixture over the crotch of the panty hose. The color black is used to deflect evil and is a powerful color. Use control-top panty hose because they have the property to constrict or hold in excess. Visualize any person, man or woman, whom you believe to have designs on your loved one. Then take the legs of the stockings and loop one through

the other and pull into a knot, sealing off the crotch. This should
deter anyone from making a move on your mate. Continue this visualization for nine days, adding a knot each day. At the end of the
spell the stocking legs should be bound together by nine knots. Wait
until the dark moon, and then bury the stockings to put an end to the
matter once and for all.

SPELL TO BE FORGIVEN FOR COMMITTING ADULTERY

Ingredients

> **oatmeal cookie**
> **butter**
> **bacon**

The Irish or Brehon laws, some dating back three thousand years,
made up a system of justice collected and passed on orally by Celtic
wanderers. In the seventh century the laws were written down in the
Gaelic language and ten centuries later they were banned and replaced by English common law. Most of the manuscripts were de-
stroyed but fortunately, several copies were saved and are now
protected in the libraries of Trinity College and Oxford University.

According to the Irish laws the penance for a hen straying into
someone else's garden is "one oat cake plus a side dish of butter or

bacon." If you have strayed into "someone else's garden," I suggest you do the following: Feed the offended party (your mate) three strips of bacon that you cooked yourself in a state of deep remorse or humility. The pig or wild boar was the symbol of the sacrificial god in ancient cultures from Greece through the Middle East to India. The death of the savior-god brought cleansing and renewal. To eat of his flesh offering was to become one with him, the same way Christians take in the body of Christ by eating the communion wafer.

Oat cakes were eaten in Scotland on Beltane, a holiday at the peak of spring to celebrate the sacred mating ritual of the God and Goddess. If necessary you may substitute an oatmeal cookie, but remember you must serve only *one*. The focus of this ritual is to heal and strengthen the bonds of a monogamous relationship and renew the passion between you. Hopefully after devouring this food your spouse will rise above his or her own human frailties and find it in his or her heart to forgive your "sin." It is also suggested that you purify yourself by rubbing a stick of pure butter over your entire body.

SPELL TO KEEP A WOMAN FAITHFUL

Ingredients

plastic wrap
1 string that has been bound around a whole chicken

40 twist ties
1 anklet made of diamonds and gold
(Note: The anklet is the only item in this book that can not be found
at a supermarket. Try Tiffany & Co. or Van Cleef & Arpels.)

"To keep your hen at home you shall tie a withe around her feet."
So says the Irish law. A withe is a band made of twisted, flexible
shoots, usually straw. The closest substitute you'll find in the supermarket are twist ties. Some authorities do claim the saying goes as
thus: "To keep your wife at home you shall tie a hen around her
feet." Hens are found in your supermarket's deli or meat depart-
ment. I'm not actually suggesting that you bind your wife's feet with
hens or twist ties to keep her from leaving. What I am suggesting is
that you "bind" her left ankle with an anklet made of diamonds and
gold. The manner in which she unwraps your gift will foretell her
future faithfulness to you.

Wrap the anklet in plastic wrap (it has that nice clinging quality).
Then braid forty twist ties around the chicken string, like you are
making a lanyard. Use forty ties as that represents the perfect couple
in Wicca. (Twenty fingers and twenty toes.) Make two strands of
twenty ties each and use the string as the center of the braid. Bind the
gift by tying a bow with your string of braided twist ties. Present this
package to your woman and watch closely. She must open the gift
without breaking the string. But you can not tell her to do so. If she
breaks it, it is an omen that faithfulness is not part of her nature, or
perhaps being devoted to you is not her will. To insure success, try

tying a very loose knot and giving her a long leash with lots of loop-holes. She also must open the plastic wrap without tearing it. If she tears it, she will break your heart. When the anklet is revealed, if she clasps it on herself it means she is selfish in bed or hard to satisfy. If she asks you to help fasten the clasp, rest assured that your money was well spent and that the two of you shall live happily and faithfully ever after.

SPELL TO KEEP A MAN FAITHFUL

Ingredients

>orange juice
>coriander seeds
>kitchen matches
>white taper candle
>paring knife

Although oranges induce love and marriage, it is said that drinking the juice of an orange can purify and tone down an out-of-control sex drive. Serving your man a glass of chilled o.j. each morning before he goes out into the world is equivalent to giving him a cold shower. As he heads towards the door slip your hands into his pockets and stash some coriander seeds there. They are known to insure fidelity. Kiss him and wave good-bye seductively. Then take a kitchen match, strike it on the heel of your shoe and whisper, "Be true." In your bedroom, light a white taper candle into which you have carved both your initials with a paring knife.

THE INFIDELITY TEST SPELL

Cock a doodle doo!
My dame has lost her shoe;
My master's lost his fiddling-stick,
And knows not what to do.

—*The Most Cruel and Bloody Murder Committed by an
Innkeeper's Wife* (1606)

Ingredients

**Corn Flakes cereal
whole milk
7 strawberries
1 banana**

You love him, yet you want to kill him. You know he's having an affair, yet you can't prove it. Will he dump her? Will he dump you? You don't know, you can't tell—here's what to do. When your husband rises and enters the kitchen, set a box of Corn Flakes firmly on the table right in front of his face. Let him look at the logo on the box: a rooster or cock, the symbol of the male. The ancient Hebrew and Arabian word for cock is *sekhvi* from the word *sakho,* meaning "seeing" the approach of the morning. There is even a morning prayer: "Blessed be the One who hath given the *sekhvi* understanding to distinguish between the day and the night."

Let that cock be the first thing he sees. In fact, serve him breakfast in bed. Show it to him before he has his morning coffee. Let him open his eyes to the subtle reminder for him to distinguish between day/lightness/goodness and night/darkness/evil. Ask him how he slept as you pour the Corn Flakes into a bowl. Corn divination was practiced by the Aztecs. It is good to ask him questions in front of a bowl of Corn Flakes. If he is telling the truth most of the Corn Flakes on the top of the bowl will be whole. If he is lying most of them will be broken. Ask him if he's still seeing his secretary. Or perhaps the woman upstairs in 6C? Begin to peel the banana. Tell him that you would prefer it if he stopped seeing her. As you slice the banana into the bowl, casually mention something you read about John Bobbitt in the *National Enquirer* while you were waiting in the checkout line at the supermarket. Give him a moment to see the light of day.

Now gently kiss him on the forehead and tell him you love him as you drop seven strawberries into the bowl. Strawberries are sacred to the Yoruban goddess Erzuli. She grants love wishes for women, and mends marriages and homes. She also delivers retribution to cheating husbands. Silently speak your heart to her. Finally pour the milk over the fruit and cereal. Milk is the symbol for the Great Mother, giver and nurturer of all life on Earth. Tell him to think of the children. Sit quietly and watch him eat his cereal. If the last piece of fruit to enter his mouth is a banana he will slip and fall. Within one year he will leave you for the other woman. If it is a strawberry, he will end his affair and remain faithful to you. If both fruits appear together in the last spoonful, he will never leave you and claim to be eternally devoted, but will continue to cheat behind your back. (In which case I say dump the bum!)

Protection and House Blessing

SPELL FOR SERIOUS PROTECTION

Ingredients

Beer
salted pretzels

No, I'm not kidding! Taking a bath in beer is said to remove the *malochio,* or evil eye. Fill the tub with water and add a quart of beer. Sit in the tub for at least ten minutes and splash the water over your head and arms. You can use a glass tumbler or even a paper cup to spill the water over you. I also recommend complete immersion at least three times. Keep your eyes open. When you get out of the tub let yourself air-dry and wrap yourself in a white towel or bathrobe. In her book, *Spiritual Cleansing,* Draja Mickaharic recommends praying the twenty-third Psalm at this point. I recommend relaxing on the couch and eating three salted pretzels. Make sure they are the old-fashioned knotted kind. Pretzel sticks will not do here. The pretzel's shape has been sacred since the ancient Celts. It is very protective and symbolizes the birth of the sun. Pretzels or Bretzels were originally eaten on the winter solstice. Its circle represents the sun and the twisted cross in the center depicts the four seasons. Picture the warmth and light of the sun around you, chasing away all negativity and darkness as the pretzel enters your stomach.

SPELL TO WARD OFF THE EVIL EYE

Ingredients

   whole raw fish
   sea salt or kosher salt
   blue plate

Fish are known to be very protective. Because they live in deep water they are said to be immune to the *malochio,* the *eyin harah,* the evil eye. In most matriarchal cultures, the fish symbolized the womb of the mother goddess. The Greek word *delphos* means both fish and womb. Most associated with fertility, the womb is also the place of protection and safety. In later times, the fish became a symbol for Christ. *Ichthus,* another Greek word meaning fish, is actually an acronym for "Jesus Christ, Son of God, Savior."

Take a fresh fish. Cut its eyes out and place them on a blue dish. Surround the eyes in a circle of salt. Hold the plate above your head with both hands and allow your arms to spiral gently in a clockwise direction. Imagine blue waters of protection washing over you and the eyes of God and Goddess watching over you. Spend at least ten minutes on this meditation. Then rinse the plate's contents down the drain with warm water and picture all evil being washed down the drain as well. There is also an ancient Hebraic custom of eating fish heads or fish eyes at the new year to bring protection and prosperity.

SABRINA'S SPELL FOR PROTECTION WHILE FLYING

Ingredients

  turmeric
  wishbone from a turkey
  feather duster
  bunch of ripe bananas

There's an old witches' adage: If a spell rhymes, it has power. If a rhyming spell is repeated three times it will come to be. Turmeric is sacred to winged Mercury, the ruler of the air. It also can be used when you are in a pickle. The Native American word for turkey is the same word used for eagle. What better magical symbol could there be for graceful flight? Feather dusters again evoke the image of wings, birds, safety, and expertise in flight. A duster is the name of a plane and feather dusters are used to clear away nasty clutter. They help clean up a situation. If anything were to go wrong mechanically with the plane, this spell will insure it is caught and cleaned up before you board. Bananas are ruled by Mars, the god of energy, and by the element of air. They grow upwards, reaching toward the sky. The magical properties of bananas include warding off negativity, bringing luck, and invoking spiritual forces. Here's the spell: Take the feather duster and brush it along the floor, then raise it up through the air and gently brush it down again on the ground. Begin chanting the spell as you do so.

> I pray the flight is safe and sound
> from taking off till touching ground.
> God on the airfare give me a really great deal
> and may the only safety hazard be the meal.
> That is why I'll pack a lunch
> one banana, no, a bunch.

Drop the wishbone through the air into a pile of powdered turmeric. Dust the turmeric off of the wishbone. Pick it up, blow on it, rub it for good luck, and place it in your back pocket. Make a wish for safety as you take your seat and buckle up. Oh, and remember to pack the bananas in your carry-on luggage.

APARTMENT HUNT SPELL

Ingredients

> **tinfoil**
> **cinnamon**
> **salt**
> **sugar**
> **bread**
> **pennies**

Spread a sheet of tinfoil across an altar or table. Stand a loaf of bread on its end. Make a roof over it with another sheet of tinfoil. Surround the bread with a circle of salt and a second circle of sugar. Take five pennies and insert them in the loaf. As you do so visualize the location you desire, the type of space you want, the price you want to pay, the date by which you need to find or occupy it, and finally, while inserting the last penny, visualize your new home being safe and protected. It is best to begin this spell on a new moon and continue putting energy into it until the moon is full. Sprinkle a pinch of cinnamon on top of the tinfoil roof for added luck and quick results. The foil serves as a magnet to draw the home you desire to you.

When moving into a new home there is a beautiful Jewish custom of bringing in bread, salt, and sugar. The bread insures you never go hungry, the salt is for protection and purification, and the sugar or candy is to make your life sweet. It is also luckiest to move in on a Tuesday and according to my granny, always enter with the right foot first! Keeping pennies (heads up) in the corners of the room will bless your home with prosperity. If you are looking to buy a house, co-op, or condo, modify the spell by adding a third circle of clam shells. You will need one shell to represent every ten thousand "clams" you intend to shell out.

To sell or rent property, separate a crab from its shell and use the shell as the foundation of the spell. Lay it under the bread. Also begin the ritual with the pennies in the bread. Complete the ritual by pulling the pennies out and putting them in your right pocket. Visualize the five things you need to happen to close the deal.

Note: Do not use a mock crab or you may end up receiving a phony check or renting to bad tenants who fool you with their fake credentials.

HOUSE BLESSING RITUAL

Ingredients

1 new broom
floral or spice carpet deodorizer
room freshener
white taper candle
spring water

A home can be spiritually cleansed as it is being physically cleansed, providing the proper energies and visualizations are utilized. Take a new broom on the new moon and sweep counterclockwise around the whole house. Sweep all negativity out the front door. Now you are ready to fill your home with positive energy.

The consecration of a space using the four elements (earth, air, fire, and water) is an ancient form of ritual blessing. Witches traditionally use salt as a symbol of the earth element. Herbs and roots can also be sprinkled to symbolize the earth element. In ancient Persia the sprinkling of spices on rugs was practiced to bring prosperity. The modern version of this antiquated ritual can be accomplished with any floral or spice carpet deodorizer. In many ways it is more functional than the sprinkling of salt. Let it sit for at least forty minutes before vacuuming. Visualize the sweet spices filling your home with health, wealth, and love. Again, this is magic, not just deodorizing. The earth element brings grounding and earthly things into your home. Next go clockwise around the house with your favorite room freshener scent, the supermarket equivalent to incense. It represents the air, which you want to be sweet and clear. Third is the element of fire. Take a white taper candle, light it, and carry it around the house clockwise, lighting up all the dark corners. Next, the element of water. Take a bowl of spring water clockwise around the home sprinkling some in all four corners. This clears the emotional life within the house and invokes love. Finally sweep again, clockwise, to seal the space and lock in all the positive energy you have raised.

SPELL TO WARD OFF NOSY NEIGHBORS

Ingredients

> **red wine vinegar**
> **bay leaves**
> **cinnamon**
> **salt**
> **key from a sardine can**
> **small mirror**

Remember Gladys in *Bewitched*? Do you have a busybody living next door to you? Here's what to do. Make a mixture using one cup of red wine vinegar, nine bay leaves, a teaspoon of cinnamon, and three pinches of salt. This is an old banishing formula from the witches' book of shadows. Use the key from a sardine can to stir the mixture. The key symbolizes the nature of the relationship, since unfortunately in modern urban settings our homes are thrust right on top of one another and we live packed together like sardines in a can. The key is also an ancient tool witches used to conduct magical energy. Remember Benjamin Franklin using the key on the kite to harness the electricity in lightning? (Franklin, by the way, was a Freemason and known to be a member of a secret magical order.) One of the eight tools of the witches is the athame or double-edged blade. It is used to represent the will. A key was and often still is substituted for an athame. Hold the key in your right hand, and as you stir the brew, chant,

> Busybody, keep away from me.
> Mind your business. So mote it be.

"So mote it be" is the witches' equivalent to "amen" and is usually said at the end of spells to give them power. The literal meaning is "so may it be" or "may it come to pass."

This is a great formula to stop gossip or slander as well. Now take a small mirror and dip it in the brew. Place the mirror in a corner of one of your windows or by your front door. If you have a mirrored peephole on the door, you should splash the mixture over it. Mirrors deflect negative energy from us and also keep people from seeing anything but their own business.

THE AMERICAN WAY SPELL

Ingredients

fresh or dried corn
popcorn

Corn brings prosperity to the home. Hanging dried corn outside the house attracts wealth. Eating corn on a full moon will increase your income. As you pop corn yell out a wish or blessing you would like to bring into your life each time you hear a kernel pop. This is a wonderful ritual to do with your whole family. It is especially good

for children, helping them to reinforce the positive and not be afraid
to go after what they want in life.

NATIVE AMERICAN HOUSE BLESSING OR CREATING SACRED SPACE

Ingredients

>corn starch or dried corn
>beans
>squash

Corn, beans, and squash are referred to by the Iroquois Indians as
the three life-sustaining sisters. To bless your home simply place a
large bowl of dried corn, dried beans, and squash gourds on your
kitchen or dining room table. This blessing is most effective in Sep-
tember, the month of the harvest. These foods can also be served and
eaten (fresh) to bless your family.

To consecrate or bless a new dwelling, roast some squash seeds
and mix them with dried beans and dried corn kernels in a bowl.
Sprinkle some in all the corners of the dwelling. You can also substitute corn starch for corn kernels. Flour is often sprinkled for consecration and dedication. Corn starch has twice the thickening power
of flour. As you sprinkle this mixture visualize the space filling with
positive energy, protection, and prosperity.

Lexa Roséan

KITCHEN WITCH MAGIC

Ingredients

> **rope of garlic, onions, or peppers**
> **baking soda**
> **bay leaves**
> **broom**

The hearth has always been known as the most sacred area of the home. The hearth is where the cooking was done. It was the nurturing center of the home, sacred to all the household gods and goddesses. If you are lucky enough to have a wood-burning stove adjoining your kitchen you understand its meaning as a gathering place—it's the warmest place in the home. Even if you have a fireplace in your home, the kitchen still will be considered the modern-day hearth. It was customary to hang a broom beside the hearth to bless and protect it. Keeping a broom in your kitchen will energize it and keep it clean.

Hanging ropes of garlic, onions, or dried peppers in the kitchen prevents accidents and food poisoning, and absorbs all negative energy. Do not eat any vegetables set aside for protective purposes. Placing an onion in the windowsill also will absorb negative energy. Replace every few months. Putting an open box of baking soda in the refrigerator clears it of negativity and also serves as an odor eater. Just as baking soda is used in laboratories to neutralize acids, it is used in magic spells to neutralize negative energy. Bay leaves added to a soup protect the family. Placed in the cupboards they drive away evil and are also a natural roach deterrent.

I remember in the seventies it became very popular to hang kitchen witches above the sink or stove. My mother and aunts all gave them to each other. A kitchen witch is a small doll with a pointed hat riding on a broomstick. The little broom is usually made out of sacred wood such as heather or cinnamon or sandalwood. If made correctly, the cloth dolls should be stuffed with sweet-smelling spices. The witch's influence in the kitchen was much desired as it brought luck and protection to the most important room in the home.

HOME SECURITY SPELL

Ingredients

> **bucket of warm water**
> **2 tablespoons vinegar**
> **black pepper**
> **salt**
> **oregano**
> **ammonia**
> **blue or white sponge**

To protect your home from burglary, fill a bucket with warm water. Add two tablespoons of vinegar, three shakes of black pepper, three pinches of salt, and a drop of ammonia. All these ingredients combined serve as protection and a repellent of evil. Throw in a dash of oregano for peace of mind. Wash the windows from the outside of the house. Wipe down all doorknobs. Finish by splashing the water over your front porch and under the doormat. For apartment dwellers with carpeted hallways, just sprinkle the water outside your door or put it in a spray bottle and mist.

CAR SECURITY SPELL

Ingredients

> **mink oil**
> **dried cranberries**
> **mustard seeds**
> **zipper food storage bag**
> **rice or dried corn or wheat germ**

Witches commonly make magic using herbs and potions that are added all together in a bag known as a *ouanga*. Here is the supermarket equivalent of a *ouanga* bag. Take a clean zipper food storage bag. Blow in it for luck, since by adding your breath you employ what is known as sympathetic magic, a personal magical link with the spell. Now add up the numbers of your license plate. Include letters too. (For instance, the letter A = 1, the letter B = 2, and so on.) Now add the digits of the total number together. (Example: If the total number is 163, 1 + 6 + 3 = 10. 1 + 0 = 1.) Your final number will end up being between one and nine. Add that many mustard seeds to the bag. This will protect you from any trouble with the law, i.e., speeding tickets. It also helps to avoid accidents.

If your car is American-made, add nine pieces of dried corn. If it's Japanese, add nine grains of uncooked rice. European-made, add a teaspoon of wheat germ. This insures that your car will sustain you and run smoothly. Now take six dried cranberries and rub them with mink oil. Cranberries are sacred to Mars in his warrior aspect. Coating the cranberries with mink oil is akin to giving Mars his armor and cloaking device. Mink oil contains lanolin, which is used to seal off the auric field and cloak the magician. Minks are fierce animals and, according to Native American legend, the mink's motto is "Don't bother me and I won't bother you!" The magical equivalent to a car alarm, dried cranberries rubbed with mink oil protect your car from thieves and make it invisible to them. It is important to note which section of the parking lot you are in when you drive to the supermarket as sometimes the car may become invisible to you, too. Add the cranberries to the bag. If you frequently drive with children, add three pieces of cereal or dried pasta that is star or crescent moon shaped. These will add protection and soothe your nerves while on the road. As you seal the zipper on your *ouanga* bag, visualize your car being blessed and protected in every way possible. Hang the bag from the rearview mirror with a twist tie or red shoestring or place on the floor under the driver's seat.

SQUAT SPELL

Ingredients

   chocolate bar

Squat has been a closely guarded secret in Manhattan for decades. She is the Goddess of parking spots. The invocation to her goes as follows: "Squat, Squat, find me a legal spot." In order to remain in her good graces it is customary to leave her an offering of a bar of chocolate once she has given you a spot. Simply leave the chocolate between your front wheel and the curb. It is also customary to taste one bite of the chocolate yourself. There are many legends about gods or goddesses being poisoned by offerings. So as a sign of good faith, always taste the first bite. *P.S.* Those who have offended Squat have often returned to their cars to find tickets on the windshield. More unlucky offenders get their cars towed away. Whether *you* believe it or not, 'tis always wise to honor Squat!

DATING AND ENTERTAINMENT

HOT DATE SPELL

Ingredients

> **garlic**
> **plum tomatoes**
> **olive oil**
> **basil**

Believe it or not, garlic is an aphrodisiac. In the Talmud, a compilation of the oral law of the Jews written in Palestine and in Babylon in the fifth and sixth centuries, men are instructed to eat garlic to increase their virility. The trick to garlic is getting both parties to ingest it; then the breath will no longer be offensive. Roasted garlic with fresh basil leaves and plum tomatoes can be served to a shy date. Tomatoes are sacred to the love goddess Venus, while garlic and basil belong to the sexy god Mars. Combining Venus and Mars foods will create a magnetic pull between the sexes. In general, the use of Venusian foods will attract romance and love. The use of Martian foods will encourage lust and sex. Use equal amounts if you want to balance these energies. Use more of one if you feel that aspect needs to be enhanced.

Slice the tomatoes and use your thumb to smear olive oil on them while fantasizing about what you'd like to do with your dinner guest. Each part of the body is ruled by a different planet or astrological sign; the thumb belongs to Venus. You can also use your thumb to spread the roasted garlic on the basil leaves or the tomato slices. It is even more effective to let your date suck the garlic off your thumb as you visualize how you would like the evening to end. After the meal your fantasies will be fulfilled.

BEWITCHING BATH

Ingredients

> **oranges**
> **fresh mint leaves**

This bath is guaranteed to turn you into a god or goddess of love. Simply fill the tub with warm water and add five whole navel oranges and a bunch of fresh mint leaves. Get in the tub. Peel the oranges and squeeze the juice into the bath water. Rub the fruit into your hair and skin. Eat a few slices to anoint yourself internally. Do the same with the mint: Rub it into the body and hair and chew on a leaf or two. You should be physically clean before taking this bath. Do not soap off when you are done. Let your body and hair air-dry. Now dress for your date. The combination of orange and mint will make you irresistible.

SPELL TO INFLUENCE PEOPLE AT PARTIES

Ingredients

   mixed nuts
   limes
   pigs in a blanket

   Nuts make people talk. Putting mixed nuts out at a party can help your guests break the ice and converse with each other. Nuts can also be used to get information from people. As you put the nuts out, hold the bowl in your hand and think very clearly about what kind of talking you wish to invoke for your party. The best nuts for business are peanuts, almonds, brazil nuts, cashews, pecans, macadamia nuts, and pistachios. Serve walnuts or hazelnuts to initiate more esoteric conversations. Brazil nuts and pistachios are also good to break the ice between potential lovers.

Limes can be used to influence or control people. Serving them in punch or as a garnish in drinks can help win people over. Make sure to squeeze them with the proper intent into the boss's or prospective client's drink.

Pigs in a blanket are little hotdogs rolled in dough. Dough has the ability to shape or give form to things. As you prepare the little "blankets," carve messages into them with a small knife. Roll over the messages with a rolling pin. In this way they will become embedded in the dough. Think of planting ideas into your guests' minds. Make the messages simple. For example, if you are holding a Tupperware party you need only carve the word *buy* into your blankets. Maybe it's just the words *have fun.* Perhaps you are anxious about a particular subject and how you will broach it to your guests. Let the dough sit and as it rises, visualize your ideas being effortlessly raised at the party. As the blankets bake, see your final desired outcome of the party being achieved.

TELEPHONE SPELLS

To Stop Someone from Calling

Ingredients

> **stick of butter or margarine**
> **peppercorns**

Butter or margarine can be used to soften or tone down a situation that has become unbearable. Pepper is used to put pressure on or control a person or situation. The combination of the two is used to stop obsessive behavior, cure anger, or to influence someone to forget about you and gently turn their energies elsewhere. This spell can be used to deter nosy mothers-in-law, ex-lovers, daughters' boyfriends, or even bill collectors from calling. Simply carve your telephone number into a stick of butter. Turn the stick over and write the name of the person or company that annoys you with telephone calls on the flip side. Place the butter stick on a dish and surround it with a circle of peppercorns. Place the dish by the phone and leave it there until the butter melts and loses its shape. The thought of calling you will melt from the person's mind.

To Get Someone to Call

Ingredients

   cotton ball
   fennel seeds
   oregano
   dill seeds
   caraway seeds

An old Southern legend claimed that if a piece of cotton stuck to a dress, a letter would be received. The shape of a letter seen in the cotton would be the initial of the person who would write. Begin by holding a cotton ball in your lap and shaping it into the initial of the person you wish to call you. Place the cotton under the phone. Sprinkle a circle of fennel, oregano, dill, and caraway seeds around the cotton. These are all spices associated with the planet Mercury, which rules communication. Visualize that person picking up a phone and calling you. I have known this spell to work within ten minutes. You should give it at least three days, though. The more energy and visualization you put into it, the quicker the results.

SPELL TO RECONCILE FRIENDS

Ingredients

> **empty cylinder from paper towel roll or toilet paper roll**
> **2 sugar cubes**
> **baking soda**

Remember making walkie-talkies or microphones out of paper towel rolls when you were a kid? Funny how a seemingly useless item can serve as a form of communication once its primary role as a paper dispenser has been fulfilled. Take a paper towel roll and write the names of the dueling friends on opposite ends. Use a blue pen, since blue is the color of forgiveness and peace. Fill the roll with two tablespoons of baking soda to absorb the negative energy between them. Then add two sugar cubes to sweeten the relationship. Cup your hands over the ends of the roll and shake. When you feel you have raised enough energy, clap your hands together, smashing the cardboard. Picture the two parties meeting halfway and reconciling.

THE DATE-FROM-HELL SPELL

Ingredients

bowl of turnips

Do you have a fatal attraction in your life? According to the folklore of the Ozark Mountains, serving a bowl of turnips to someone you despise will cause him or her to fall out of love with you and end unwanted advances towards you. Although the turnip is a root vegetable with down-to-earth attributes, it is ruled by Neptune, the dreamy planet named after the god of the sea. Blessed with both watery and earthy elements, turnips act as illusion breakers. They can also be used to dispel nightmares whether they happen to occur in a waking or dreaming state. Turnips are also used to send messages and to help people integrate information.

Are you tired of dating the wrong types? Can't seem to meet anyone decent? To ward off the potential date from hell, carry a turnip in your purse or pocket whenever you go to a bar or party. This will deliver a very powerful message and keep Mr. or Ms. Wrong from even approaching you.

QUICK-FIX SPELLS

Ingredients

assorted sodas
cinnamon doughnuts
cup of coffee
assorted hard candy
assorted flavor chewing gum
nuts

Perhaps you don't have a lot of time to spend in the supermarket. Here are some quick-fix spells for those people who only have time for the under-ten-items checkout lane or a fast dash into the 7-Eleven.

A cup of coffee and a cinnamon doughnut can bring success and concentration, or prepare you for a hard day's work. They make a perfect treat to bring into the office and eat before you begin your day. Coffee increases your capacity to work. Cinnamon grants swiftness of action, and bestows that mystery element of success known as *luck*. The combination of coffee and cinnamon can make you more authoritative, influential, and help beat out competition.

Coca-Cola improves concentration and creativity, and speeds up the mental process. Originally the beverage contained trace elements of cocaine, and although it is no longer an ingredient, its properties continue to work on a vibrational level. The beverage also contains caffeine, derived from kola nuts. Native to Africa, these nuts were chewed to open the mind for vision quests.

Root beer can alleviate depression. Its derivative herb, sarsaparilla, is brewed in teas by witches to bring happiness.

Nuts are prosperity foods and were actually used as legal tender in ancient civilizations. (So was salt). Nuts can also improve your verbal skills and can be eaten if you want to charm or convince someone of something. Ginger is always used to speed up and empower love or money spells. Drink ginger ale and eat salted nuts for success with negotiations and sales. Raspberry ginger ale brings quick results in love. Ginger adds the speed and raspberries are sacred to Venus, the goddess of love. Black cherry soda gives self confidence. In fact, any cherry-flavored food will improve your self-worth or self-respect as cherries are the fruit of self-love.

I recommend carrying assorted gum or candy in case you are ever in a pinch. Suppose you are walking down the street and you see Mr. or Ms. Right approaching? No time for a Bewitching Bath! (see Dating and Entertainment section) Quickly pop an orange candy and a piece of peppermint gum into your mouth. Instant irresistibility!

If you find yourself in an unsafe neighborhood or situation, chew a piece of wintergreen gum for protection. Native North Americans would rub the leaves on their bodies before going to battle to give them vigor and protection.

Spearmint leaves were chewed for mental stimulation and used in folk remedies to clear the head. Spearmint gum is good to chew when you are losing an argument, or need to be quick with a witty or sharp comeback. It can also be chewed to do well on exams.

The exotic pineapple is a fruit of prosperity. Combined with cinnamon it will quicken your earning power. Wrap a pineapple-flavored candy in a piece of cinnamon gum to bring money and fast luck.

Cinnamon gum with a cherry candy can bring you good luck on a job interview. Cinnamon's success and influence vibrations coupled with the self-confidence properties of cherry will make you unbeatable.

Lime-flavored candies are good if you want to be a quick-talking salesperson, as lime is used to dominate or influence others to your way of thinking. Add a cinnamon or ginger candy to lime if you need to close a deal quickly and are dealing with stubborn or slow-moving clients.

Coconut or lemon candies are good purifiers when you are feeling jinxed or vexed. Most voodoo protection or uncrossing formulas will call for either coconut or lemon to clear away obstacles, although an old New Orleans recipe combines coconut, lemon, and cherry for a powerful love attraction spell. I suggest sucking the lemon and coconut candies first while visualizing all obstacles in your path disappearing. Then add the cherry and approach the person you wish to attract.

Throughout this book I have explained the magical properties of various foods and herbs. Many (especially fruits) are available as flavorings in soft drinks and snacks. Use your imagination and creativity to create your own quick-fix spell based on the information in this book.

Prosperity and Success

LOAVES AND FISHES PROSPERITY SPELL

Ingredients

5 sesame seed buns
2 cans tuna fish
1 onion
celery
lettuce
lemon
mayonnaise

Does the cost of living make you anxious? Worried about not making enough to feed your family? This spell wards off poverty and insures prosperity. It is no coincidence that we use the words *bread* or *dough* to refer to money. Yet man does not live by bread alone.

Fish, along with being protective, are a symbol of prosperity in many ancient cultures. According to the gospel of Matthew, Jesus fed about five thousand men plus the women and children with five loaves of bread and two fishes. After everyone ate and was satisfied, twelve baskets were passed around to collect the leftovers. According to Herodotus, the Greek historian, the Egyptian pharaohs spent nine tons of gold to buy onions for the slaves who built the pyramids.

Sometimes we forget the preciousness of things that seem quite ordinary. For instance, mayonnaise, although now commonplace, was originally considered a very select French sauce. Let's examine the components of *la mayonnaise:* Lemon and salt are used to purify and cleanse. Vinegar drives away evil forces and eggs absorb negativity. Sugar sweetens life and the main ingredient, soybeans, are known as the "bean of good fortune" in Chinese and Japanese lore. On the Japanese New Year soybeans are scattered around the home to bring prosperity. Mayonnaise with all its magical ingredients can be used to chase away poverty and to draw blessings and abundance. Celery and lettuce are associated with male fertility gods and will help you to be fruitful and multiply. Eating them can produce a state of peace. Also their green color makes them money-drawing or prosperity foods. Sesame was once known as the most fruitful of all plants. Lemons with their vibrant yellow color invoke solar energy and bring happiness and peace of mind.

Now here's the miracle. Open the cans of fish. Add diced onions (purple to add power to the spell), chopped celery, a squeeze of lemon juice, and a few heaping tablespoons of mayonnaise. Mix well and spread on buns. Add a few leaves of lettuce to each sandwich. Cut each in half. Cut in half again, making twenty little sandwiches in all. The number twenty is very magical. It represents a complete person—ten fingers and ten toes. Share these sandwiches with your family or friends. As you eat, visualize enough food, money, etc., to make each person feel happy, whole, and complete always. At the end of the meal gather together twelve pinches or crumbs from the sandwiches in a basket and place them as an offering outside under a tree. As you thank God and Goddess imagine there always being enough leftovers. The principle of prosperity teaches that there is always enough for all. We need not deprive another human being or the Earth itself in order to meet our own needs.

SPELL FOR SUCCESS

Ingredients

    allspice
    basil
    bay leaves
    cinnamon
    cloves
    nutmeg

These herbs are popular ingredients in incense formulas burned for success and money. Allspice and clove are both ruled by Jupiter, the planet of luck and business expansions. Because of their green color, bay and basil are said to attract money. Basil is usually used in love spells but also can be employed to tap into the drive and ambition attributes of Mars. Bay is ruled by the sun and most often is used for healing or protection; however, an American folklore tradition holds that the person who finds a bay leaf in his or her soup will have a wish fulfilled. In ancient Greece, wreaths of bay laurel were used to crown the Olympic winners.

The earliest documentation of cinnamon was found in Chinese writings dating back to 2700 B.C. It was prized in biblical times by both Jews and Arabs and used as an anointing oil in the holy temples. Ruled by the sun, it was considered as precious as frankincense and gold. Modern-day witches add cinnamon to love, healing, success, and money spells. It is an all-purpose holy herb. Combining bay and cinnamon will attract fame.

Ruled by Jupiter and Mercury, nutmeg is traditionally taken in trace amounts to awaken psychic or intuitive powers. In a modern voodoo spell, a hole is made in a nutmeg, filled with liquid mercury, sealed with wax, and the nutmeg is carried for gambling luck. Success often comes through following your intuition and taking a gamble.

Fill a pot with all these herbs. Add spring water and simmer on the stove. Witches incorporate the four elements into their spells to manifest success on all four planes. The element of air concerns the realization of our thoughts or plans. The element of fire represents our desires and the actions that will lead to their fulfillment. The element of water symbolizes our emotional well-being, and the element of earth stands for the physical manifestation of our desired end. The herbs represent the earth element. The stove is the fire element. Adding the spring water gives you the water element, and the steam the brew releases as you cook it creates the air element. Let the fragrance fill your home to attract successful vibrations. You can also fill your pockets with these herbs to insure success out in the world.

CHANGO MACHO MONEY SPELL

Ingredients

   apples
   cinnamon
   coconut
   red taper candle
   red or red-and-white tablecloth

Chango Macho is the Cuban-African god of wealth and business. He is also the god of *iwa-pêlê,* or "good character." Apples, cinnamon, and coconut are all foods that attract his energy. You can eat these foods to make yourself powerful in business and to build good character. As everyone scrambles around in the rat race, it is wise to remember that a good reputation is often the key to success!

It is customary to leave these foods as offerings for Chango on an altar. Simply clear a space on a table or countertop and cover it with a red or red-and-white tablecloth. These are the colors of Chango. Light a red taper candle and place the apples, coconut, and cinnamon before it. After one week you may remove the food and dispose of it. By the way, Chango also loves a good cigar. Light the cigar in front of the altar and blow the smoke over the candle and food. Many supermarkets still sell tobacco. Check it out.

MONEY DRAWING SPELLS

Ingredients

**chocolate milk or chocolate bars
gingersnaps or cinnamon buns**

Chocolate is ruled by Mars and can be used for either sex or money magic. The source of chocolate, cacao or cocoa beans were once used as currency. In the same way that chocolate gives your system a quick sugar rush, it will also give your pocket a quick cash supply.

Sacred to the mother goddess, milk is universally recognized as a source of nourishment. It is best to drink milk to draw money when the moon is full. According to witches, the full moon is when the goddess grants all we need to sustain us. In the Old Testament milk and honey symbolize abundance. Drink hot chocolate sweetened with honey during the new-to-full-moon period to steadily increase your income.

Ginger or cinnamon can bring money to you very quickly. They are both used for luck and swiftness. Hot and fiery spices, they tend to burn up what they draw as quickly as they attract it. Eat these snacks at midday to increase your earning power and luck (especially if you work on commission), or use them towards the end of the month when you need that extra cash to make ends meet. This spell will not draw a lot of money but it will draw it fast.

Ingredients

Earl Grey tea
green food coloring

Earl Grey tea is made with bergamot, a spice used for drawing money. Drink a cup of Earl Grey first thing in the morning to increase your earning power or add four tea bags to a tub of hot water along with half a capful of green food coloring. Bathe for ten to fifteen minutes while visualizing the amount of money you need. Cup your hands and fill them with the green bathwater. Imagine your hands are filled with cash.

Ingredients

1 can of crushed pineapple or fresh pineapple
fresh blackberries or blackberry jam

grapes or grape jelly
any nut butter
oat bread

Green grapes are eaten to attract money and in general all fruits of the vine are said to spread wealth. Visualize your income climbing and your business branching out as you eat blackberries or grapes. Because of its spiny exterior and sweet juicy interior, the pineapple teaches us that beneath hard backbreaking work lie sweet rewards. In Cuba, Puerto Rico, and Hawaii it is considered an important harvest crop, and island lore honors the fruit as a sacred symbol of wealth. Make a fruit salad with crushed pineapple, blackberries, and grapes to increase your income.

Most nuts have money drawing properties. In several ancient civilizations nuts actually were used as legal tender. Almonds, brazil nuts, cashews, walnuts, and pine nuts can be eaten to draw cash. Pecans can be eaten for employment. Pistachios and macadamia nuts are known as "rich nuts" and should be eaten to draw large sums of money. This brings me to the ever popular peanut. Peanuts were originally cultivated by the ancient Mayans in South America. They were considered a food of fertility and wealth because they grew and developed underground in the belly of Mother Earth. In the United States, the peanut became known as the "poor man's nut" and was associated with slave crops. However, George Washington Carver greatly improved the economy of the South by convincing farmers to plant peanut crops. He discovered the ever precious peanut oil and peanut butter, thus proving the innate wealth hidden within the peanut.

All grains are considered to be prosperity foods. The pagans of Bavaria and Bohemia would fashion an "oats goat" out of the last sheath of oat to be harvested. The oats goat would be carried through the town and would dance in all the houses to bring abundance and would dance with all the women to bring fertility. Food and money were also given to the oats goat to win his favor.

Prepare any nut butter sandwich on oat bread with blackberry or grape jelly. Eat to draw money on a steady and consistent level. Use pistachio nut butter on the sandwich or add macadamia nuts to the fruit salad if you need money to buy something extravagant.

Ingredients

alfalfa sprouts

It is said that eating alfalfa sprouts before going to the bank will help you get a loan. It is also believed to attract generous investors. This is a relatively modern myth and, until this point, a closely guarded secret in underground wiccan circles. The legend goes as follows: Shortly after the leguminous herb was introduced into every health salad served in the Golden State, a bleary-eyed and bankrupt screenwriter exclaimed "Eureka," mistaking the sprouts for the arms of a philanthropist holding out cash. In his excitement, he knocked over his table, spilling his sprouted salad upon the lap of the man sitting next to him. He was promptly thrown out of the restaurant and arrested for disturbing the peace and not having enough money to cover his check. Meanwhile, the man at the next table sat quietly eating his sprouts, not even bothering to brush off the alfalfa that had landed in his lap. The next day his project was fully funded.

Alfalfa comes from the Arabic word *alfasfasah,* meaning "the best kind of fodder," and its crops greatly enrich the soil. If you need "fodder" for a pet project eat alfalfa sprouts. Let some fall into your lap to draw investors. As you ingest them look at the long green arms of the shoots and visualize the bank "branch" sprouting dollar bills.

SPELL TO SAVE MONEY

Ingredients

yams

Yams are blessed with the property of grounding. To eat them or any other root vegetable can have stabilizing effects. To secure or save a specific amount of money, carve the amount into a yam. Cook and eat it. When yams are heated their candy, or honey, is released. As you eat it imagine your money sticking to you. You can also create a yam "piggy" bank spell. If you are artistically inclined, carve the yam into the shape of a pig. The pig is a symbol of prosperity. Then cut a deep slit in the yam and deposit one penny for every one hundred or one thousand dollars you need to save. Let the yam sit in the sun and grow roots. On a full moon bury it in the yard. In the same way your savings will take root and grow.

SPELL TO ELIMINATE POVERTY

Ingredients

>   **sugar**
>   **salt**
>   **rice**
>   **open safety pin**

Based on a New Orleans voodoo formula, this spell will insure that you always have the staples in life. Fill a bowl with equal parts sugar, salt, and rice. Place an open safety pin in its center. Keep the bowl out in the open to eliminate poverty.

SPELL FOR INSPIRATION AND CREATIVITY

Ingredients

>   **star-shaped pasta**
>   **pine nuts or pistachios**
>   **sesame or olive oil**

basil and garlic (optional)
carbonated drinks

Pasta, pine nuts, and pistachios are all Mercury and Gemini foods that stimulate the mind and feed the creative centers of our brains. Sesame and olive are both sacred to Apollo, the god of music, art, and theatre. I suggest eating a simple bowl of star-shaped noodles or pasta with some olive or sesame oil and crushed pine nuts or pistachios to bring on a creative spell. You can go ahead and make it a pesto sauce by adding basil and garlic. The garlic will increase your drive and the basil will add the Venusian aspect of beauty and artistic appreciation.

All carbonated drinks are ruled by Gemini and can be consumed for a quick summoning of the inspirational muse.

SUCCESS IN SCHOOL SPELL

Ingredients

  rosemary
  mustard
  spearmint chewing gum

Rosemary improves the memory. I suggest seasoning your food with it while you are studying for exams. Mustard stimulates the brain, and as it is ruled by Mars, it increases our drive and ambition. Adding mustard to sandwiches can increase brain power and motivate students to improve their studies and grades. If you have crammed until the final hour and are still feeling insecure, chew a piece of spearmint gum while taking a test. Spearmint also stimulates the brain and can be used as a quick fix to help you remember information.

CHILDREN

SPELL TO CONCEIVE CHILDREN

Ingredients

pumpkins
pomegranates
figs
honey

Eating pomegranates and pumpkins is said to enhance fertility. Belief in the reproductive powers of these foods sprang from the fact that they are filled with seeds. Figs are another seedy food said to make a woman fertile. Women should eat these foods during ovulation to increase their chances of conception. Men should eat them on new moons to increase their sperm count.

There is a Yoruban goddess named Oshun who loves pumpkins. If one petitions her to bear a child, it is actually taboo to eat pumpkin or pumpkin seeds as they are her children. Simply make an offering to her of a pumpkin smothered in honey. Make sure to taste the honey before presenting the offering. One legend tells of an attempt to poison her with honey, so you must always taste it to let her know the offering is safe. Oshun is the goddess of the river so you must deliver the pumpkin to the closest river on the night of a full moon.

SPELL TO INSURE A HEALTHY BIRTH

Ingredients

    yellow squash
    corn
    butterscotch candies
    red string or ribbon

It is said that eating yellow foods or having them in a delivery room insures happiness and health for both mother and child. Yellow is the color of Oshun, the Yoruban fertility goddess. Yellow is also the color of egg yolks and therefore symbolizes the unborn child. Witches burn yellow candles called solarblasts on their birthdays to bring health and happiness in the coming year. In astrological terms, a birthday is called a solar return because it marks the sun's return to the exact degree of the Zodiac constellation under which you were born. In Mexico, it is good luck to wear yellow at the new year or when you begin something.

In the Jewish tradition the color red is used to protect the mother and child. It symbolizes the lifeblood of creation. It is traditional to tie a red string around the wrists of both mother and child or to tie a red ribbon around the crib.

SPELL TO KEEP CHILDREN HAPPY

Ingredients

   cherries
   root beer
   peanut butter and apple butter sandwiches

Cherries are the fruit of self-confidence and self-love and bring happiness. Root beer or sarsaparilla is said to induce playfulness. Peanut butter and apple butter are also self-confidence foods and give energy, health, grounding, and protection. Whole wheat or bread with grains provide more physical and mental stimulation and are healthier than white bread which weighs the physical body down. Simply feed these foods to your children as snacks or meals.

SPELL TO INSPIRE CHILDREN TO BE CREATIVE

Ingredients

circular or star-shaped cereals
circular, tubular, or spiraled pastas
carrot juice
almonds
bananas
dates

I do not suggest feeding your children all these foods in one sitting. However, adding some or all to their regular diet can increase their creative powers. All circular or star-shaped cereals promote creativity and circular, tubular, or spiraled pastas are more mentally stimulating than old-fashioned straight spaghetti. Carrot juice gives mental and physical energy and increases drive and motivation. Almonds, bananas, and dates are all ruled by the element of air, which influences our thoughts and ideas.

SPELL FOR TOO MUCH TELEVISION

Ingredients

chocolate cake rolls with white creme spiral filling

The spiral is an ancient Neolithic symbol that existed long before television. Anyone can become hypnotized looking into a spiral. It is a powerful image to use to send subliminal messages. You can use spiral-shaped pasta but I find the cake roll easier to work with. There are several spiral cake roll products in the supermarket. I have also seen a white cake roll with a jam-filled spiral center. You can use this as a substitute, but I recommend chocolate because it is a stimulant and will create excitement about receiving the subliminal message. Simply take a chocolate cake roll and carve "No TV" in the white creme spiral filling. Move the cake roll in a circular clockwise motion before your child's eyes, tempting and implanting a subliminal message at the same time. Move closer and closer until you are close enough for the child to bite into the mouthwatering treat. Once the child eats the cake roll, the message will be delivered to the child's subconscious.

SPELL TO INFLUENCE PARENTS IN YOUR FAVOR

Ingredients

ice
13 limes
sugar
a pitcher
a ballpoint pen

Okay, kids, forget the lemonade stand. Limeade is a much more powerful thirst quencher and can be used to get your way. Take thirteen whole limes. Use a ballpoint pen and write your requests on the surface of the limes. For example: "Keys to the car" or "Stay up late to watch TV." There is great magic in the alphabet and spelling things out is the first step to achieving our desires. There are thirteen full moons in a year, so witches use the number thirteen for power and luck. Now slice the limes and squeeze with all your will and might. As the lime juice falls into the pitcher, concentrate on squeezing your parents into submission. Now add sugar to sweeten up your folks and fill the pitcher with crushed ice. Ice and sugar are used to "freeze" a person into taking only positive actions toward you.

Let the pitcher stand in the sun. Sun magic—capturing the rays of the sun—is done to add success and victory to spells. As the ice melts into water, stir the brew clockwise or toward you and visualize your parents "melting down," giving in, and coming around to your way of thinking. Serve the first two glasses to your mother and/or father and sell the remaining limeade to neighborhood parents. As they drink your magic potion, visualize them doing things to make their children happy. Have fun and remember the witches' creed: "Do what ye will and harm none." (In other words, don't ask for anything that would be harmful to *yourself* or your family!)

SPELL TO PROTECT CHILDREN FROM HARM

Ingredients

  blueberries

Blueberries are ruled by the moon and are extremely protective. Sprinkle them on your children's cereal in the morning to insure their safety while they are out in the world. For extreme cases of danger, I recommend staining the body with blueberries. Perhaps you are afraid of losing your children in a custody battle or you know they are around negative influences. Marking the face or the feet in particular will steer them away from danger and bring them safely back to you. Under no circumstances must you frighten your children while doing this. Turn it into a fun game. For instance, fill the tub with blueberries and let the children stamp on them like the Italian winegrowers. In this way their feet will become stained and insure the path they walk is protected. Or let them paint protective symbols on their faces like Native American or African warriors. If this is done on a full moon its effects will last until the next full moon. So don't worry, it's okay to wash their faces after the game is done.

SPELL TO INVOKE THE INNER CHILD

Ingredients

> **macaroni and cheese**
> **popsicles**
> **angel food cake**

These ingredients are totally personalized. They were my favorites as a child, and yet they are things I would never eat today—too fattening and I'm too grown up. Maybe it's cotton candy, hotdogs, or cookie dough for you. The idea is to chose food you would never allow yourself to indulge in these days, food that takes you back to the innocent and carefree days of your childhood. Eat these foods and meditate on your inner child. Try to bring him or her out by laughing and sharing these treats. Take note of what your inner child is asking for: comfort, healing, fun, joy, security? As an adult you are now capable of providing those things for your inner child. Imagine the little you standing before the adult you and give that little one a big kiss on the forehead as you end your meditation.

SPELL FOR PETS

Ingredients

>**1 jelly jar**
>**sugar**
>**fur clipping of an animal**

While in the country one summer my hostess's dog Luna was having trouble welcoming another guest's dog into the house. I suggested a spell taught to me years ago by Lady Miw, my high
priestess. We used it to help two cats adjust to living together. Simply
take small fur clippings from both animals and put them in a jelly
jar. Add a few heaping teaspoons of sugar and water and shake.
Chant "love" or "be sweet" and shake the jar several times daily in
front of the animals. By the end of the weekend Luna had calmed
down considerably and allowed the other dog some space. Cats are
more difficult. Give the spell at least a full moon to a full moon (a
month) before giving up on it.

Luck and Legalities

LEGBA LUCK AND UNCROSSING SPELL

Ingredients

   coconut
   imitation rum (or the real thing)
   cinnamon

Legba is the lord of obstacles. Similar to the Indian god Ganesh and the Greek god Hermes, this Yoruban god helps to clear the way and remove obstacles in your path to success. Leave offerings to him on the floor by your front door. Open a coconut and fill it with a shot of rum (real or imitation). Sprinkle cinnamon on top. Ask Legba to remove all obstacles in your path to success.

Drink a shot of warm coconut milk flavored with cinnamon and rum to remove bad luck. You can add three shots of this mixture to your bathwater. Legba is also petitioned to help release you from prison.

SPELLS TO WIN AT COURT

Ingredients

> **dill**
> **coriander**
> **bell pepper**
> **spring water**

Peppers are very protective and combined with coriander and dill, they can influence judges and juries to act on your behalf. Slice a bell pepper in half. Remove the seeds. Use a green pepper if you are seeking money through legal channels, red for justice or retribution, orange for success in signing or negotiating contracts or to speed up the legal process, yellow to prove your innocence. Purple peppers, although rare, can be used for power and are recommended if you are suing large corporations, government agencies, or hospitals. Place five coriander seeds and four sprinkles of dill in the pepper. Add a piece of paper with the names of all parties involved in the court case, including yourself. Add an eighth of a cup of spring water and place in the freezer twelve days before your court date. Keep it in the freezer until the verdict has been reached. Open the freezer each day and "freeze" a victorious image of yourself in your mind's eye.

Ingredients

    chestnut
    sage
    tobacco
    black taper candle

Carefully drill or cut a hole in a chestnut. Chestnuts increase your willpower and cause others to believe you. Stuff it with a pinch of sage and a pinch of loose tobacco to make your arguments foolproof. Drip the wax of a black taper candle over the opening to seal it. Black candles are not evil. They are burned to influence, bring focus and concentration, and to absorb negative energy. They are also used to cloak information or hide secrets. When you enter the courtroom, carry this talisman in your right pocket to bring luck, believability, and a favorable verdict.

Ingredients

    a scouring pad
    tobacco
    sage
    coriander
    dill

chestnut
white or yellow taper candle

If you have been wrongfully accused of murder, take a scouring
pad and stretch it out to create little grooves in the steel wool. Stuff
loose tobacco, sage, coriander, dill, and ground chestnut into the
grooves. Steel wool is made of steel fibers. Steel is a tough alloy of
iron that contains carbon. Iron and carbon have the magical properties of invoking justice and exposing any information that stands in
the way of truth. The color white symbolizes innocence, while yellow
brings hope in place of despair. Place a white or yellow taper candle
in the center of the steel wool and let it burn completely. Make sure it
is on a nonflammable surface. Gather the whole ball of wax and
wool and bury in the ground on the new moon before your trial
begins.

Ingredients

scouring pad
tobacco
sage
coriander
dill
chestnut
lemon juice
black taper candle

If you have been rightfully accused of murder, repeat the above procedure. After filling the grooves of the steel wool, squeeze the juice of a lemon over it to absolve guilt. You must burn a black taper candle to completion. (However, you may burn blue to invoke mercy.) Then take the steel wool in your hands while the wax is still warm. Rub vigorously until your hands begin to bleed while chanting "out out damn spot." Immediately follow up with a money spell so you can afford a good attorney. Just kidding!

LUCKY SUNDAE SPELL

Ingredients

> **vanilla ice cream**
> **cinnamon sugar**
> **strawberry topping**
> **watermelon**

Fruit oils are commonly used in "horn of plenty" spells to promote luck in games of chance. Cherries, plums, lemons, and oranges are also popular symbols found on slot machines. This custom stems from the Greek myth of Amalthea, whose horn became the fruit-filled cornucopia.

Tonka beans are used in Mexico as a vanilla substitute and carried by modern-day witches for luck. Real vanilla is used in love spells but can also be ingested to win the love and favor of the gods. I have mentioned the properties of cinnamon throughout this book. It is one of the most useful spices for witches. Added to spells for healing, luck, love, and money drawing, cinnamon also makes you more psychic and is an excellent ingredient to help you divine your lucky lotto numbers.

This recipe is an adaptation of an old New Orleans favorite called Lucky Dog. The blend is traditionally made with essential oils of vanilla, watermelon, strawberry, and cinnamon and then rubbed on the hands before gambling. Take a scoop of vanilla ice cream, slices of watermelon (remove the seeds), drizzle with strawberry topping or fresh strawberries, and a dash of cinnamon sugar. Eat before gambling or playing the lotto to increase your luck.

LUCK SPELLS

Ingredients

> cotton balls
> sugar
> cotton candy
> bay leaves
> cinnamon stick

In Southern folklore, keeping a cotton ball in a bowl of sugar brings luck to your home. Cotton candy is a magical process of "spinning sugar into cotton." Many ancient cultures believed that a sweet and sticky substance brought good luck when ingested because then sweet things would stick to you. Eating cotton candy will bring you good luck. It is customary to make a wish as you pinch off a piece of cotton candy. You must hold the wish in your thoughts until the cotton candy completely dissolves in your mouth. Then the wish is said to come true.

If your bad luck concerns your teeth, I do not recommend using this or the Lucky Sundae spell. Instead try carrying two bay leaves and a cinnamon stick in your pocket. The combination of bay and cinnamon is believed to turn your luck around. Bay wards off evil or bad luck and cinnamon has been offered to win the favor of the gods since ancient Egyptian times. To turn a bad day around quickly, hold a bay leaf in one palm and sprinkle cinnamon powder in the other. Swiftly rub your palms together and crumble the bay leaf. When you feel the heat begin to generate between your palms, open your hands and let them fall to your sides. Dust your hands by quickly brushing or clapping seven times against your front pants pockets. If your clothing does not have front pockets or if you are afraid of soiling the fabric, remove your shoes and slap each foot seven times. This will lead you to where your luck is. If you are having a slow day in your place of business, place a piece of tinfoil in the center of the space. Crumble three bay leaves onto the foil. Add a fistful of cinnamon powder and seven pennies. Ball up the tinfoil and shake the mixture. Poke holes in the tinfoil ball and sprinkle around the entire area including the cash register.

WORK

JAVA MAGIC SPELL

Ingredients

that ole' black coffee

The stimulant effects of coffee were first experienced by grazing goats in Ethiopia around 1200 A.D. The goat is the symbol for Capricorn, the sign of hard work. It is traditional to have a cup of coffee before settling into one's daily work. Coffee can be used in various ways, aside from drinking it. Taking a bath in coffee (add three cups of espresso to half a tub of water) can prepare you for the hours of hard work ahead. It produces an abundance of physical energy without the side effects that drinking too much coffee can cause. Brewing coffee in a room can stimulate others to buckle down and concentrate. The smell alone will produce these effects, you need not drink it. A powder made of ground coffee and ground cinnamon can be sprinkled around a room, carried in the pockets, or dusted over your hands to produce quick and successful results. Adding a pinch of ground nutmeg to the mixture will make you lucky at the racetrack. Coffee can also be used to divine the future if it is prepared in the Turkish fashion. Boil water and add one heaping teaspoon of coffee for each cup. Add sugar. Bring to a second boil on a low flame. Take off when coffee begins to rise. When finished drinking, swirl the dregs around and turn them upside down onto a plate. The pictures formed there can be used to see the future.

CHORE SPELL

Ingredients

> **brown sponge**
> **pot of coffee**
> **coffee filters**

Take a coffee filter and write down all the chores that need to be done around the house. Now place the filter in the coffee machine and brew a pot of coffee. Let it cool and add to your husband's or boyfriend's (or wife's or girlfriend's) bathwater. Put him or her in the tub. You want your loved one to be as relaxed as possible so you can open his or her subconscious. Now sponge him or her down in the bath. Remember, sponges absorb things. You are trying to get your loved one to absorb some important information. Brown is the color for hard work and is used in candle spells to command people to perform tasks. As you wring the coffee water from the sponge over the back and shoulders casually mention all the things that need to be done around the house. This bath should give him or her the vitality and motivation to do the chores.

SPELL FOR EMPLOYMENT

Ingredients

> **spinach**
> **lettuce**
> **parsley**
> **all grains**

Spinach and lettuce are green foods and can attract money. Spinach is ruled by Jupiter, the planet of expansions and success. Lettuce is ruled by the moon. Eating spinach can make you confident and help you find a job that is a step up the ladder in your career. Lettuce can improve your intuitive edge and reveal hidden opportunities to you. Parsley is ruled by Mercury and can help open channels for those who need to network. Eating grains of any kind draws money and will give you an air of success in your interviews.

If you are interested in getting a particular job, make a parsley tea and drink it before the interview. Add three drops of lime juice. This forces others to be compelled by your words. If you add a few drops of juice from a very sweet orange, others will be charmed by you as well.

SPELL TO GET A RAISE

Ingredients

  oatmeal
  cinnamon
  walnuts
  pinch of salt

Did you know that the origin of salary is *salarium,* or "salt money," the Roman word for salt rations? Walnuts were so rare in ancient Persia that they once served as currency. Cinnamon was a favorite among the gods of ancient Egypt and Greece and offered to try to influence them to grant the requests of mortals. In ancient Germanic tribes, oats were a chief harvest grain and they believed that a divine spirit manifested itself in the grain to provide sustenance for the people. Oatmeal eaten in the morning draws money and prosperity. Prepare a bowl of oatmeal, adding walnuts. Sprinkle cinnamon on top in the shape of a dollar sign. Add a pinch of salt. Do this during a new moon cycle on the morning you ask your boss for a raise.

If you work on commission, you can eat this every morning or prepare a talisman to carry with you to increase sales. Simply take a walnut shell, add five grains of uncooked oatmeal, a pinch of salt, and sprinkle cinnamon on top in the shape of a dollar sign. Wrap the walnut shell in a dollar bill. Make sure the pyramid on the dollar is facing the outside. Carry this in your pocket or purse. (U.K. equivalent: a pound coin, Queen's head up. Put walnut on top of Queen's head.)

SPELL FOR CONCENTRATION

Ingredients

> **pumpernickel or black bread**
> **cinnamon powder**
> **cream cheese**
> **raisins**

Black is the color for deep thought or concentration. Pumpernickel or rye is sacred to Mercury and Pluto. Together they rule deep thought or contemplation. Cheese is ruled by Saturn, the most serious and focused planet. Saturn allows us to focus on long-term projects and teaches responsibility. As you spread the cream cheese over the bread, make sure you cover the bread completely. Imagine your focus and concentration being distributed evenly and smoothly, and lasting till the completion of your project. Place raisins on the bread in the shape of a circle, spiral, or five-pointed star. These are all power symbols. Raisins are ruled by both the moon and the sun and therefore strengthen the subconscious (creative and intuitive) and the conscious (logical and organizational) mind. A sprinkle of cinnamon on top will add a little fire to keep you focused. Eat before or during intense work or study periods.

SPELLS FOR LAZINESS

Ingredients

> **artichoke**
> **asparagus**
> **chili**
> **mustard**
> **all spicy foods**

These foods are all ruled by Mars, the planet of action, and Aries, the sign of initiation. If you are having trouble getting projects off the ground, add these foods to your diet. There is an especially effective spell that can be done while eating a whole artichoke. As you peel off the layers visualize yourself removing all the obstacles causing your inertia. See yourself getting to the heart of your work as you reach the heart of the artichoke. In a quick pinch, when you need to get yourself going, simply put a dab of hot mustard under your tongue. Guaranteed to stimulate the brain and body!

SPELL FOR WORKAHOLICS

Avoid bitter foods, frozen foods, and pickled or preserved foods. They are all ruled by Capricorn, the sign of hard work. Steamed foods are recommended since they are ruled by the moon and can help bring peace into your life. Ice cream is a good antidote for those who work too hard. So is seafood. But avoid lobster because unless it's shelled—it's too much work!

SPIRITUALITY

SPELL FOR MOURNERS

Ingredients

white candle or *yahrzeit* candle
eggplant
zucchini
hard-boiled egg
gefilte fish

Yahrzeit candles are special candles in a glass used to commemorate the dead. They are usually sold in supermarkets. If you can not locate one, substitute with a white taper or Sabbath candle. Burning white candles accomplishes two things. One, it sheds light for the departed soul to find their spiritual path, and two, it gives comfort, peace, and healing to the living.

Eggplant is sacred to the cemetery goddess. Eating eggplant helps you to come to terms with endings and death, while eating zucchini puts you in touch with the principle of rebirth. Zucchini is ruled by the moon and is also considered a food of comfort.

In the Jewish religion, it is customary for mourners to eat a hard-boiled egg after returning from the cemetery. The egg is a symbol of rebirth. According to a Yiddish folktale, you should eat gefilte fish after hearing of a death. It is believed to protect you from death and grant long life and happiness.

In Mexican and other Central and South American traditions, favorite foods of the deceased are left in front of a burning candle. It is believed that the departed will often visit loved ones to comfort them or to be comforted. Imagine being lost in a completely strange land and then suddenly recognizing your favorite meal. The food will help those who have crossed over locate you and will also calm the soul of the departed.

I had quite a magical event take place when my grandfather died. I was not able to attend the funeral, so I wanted to create some kind of ritual to say good-bye to him. I lit a candle and placed a picture of him next to it. Something told me to place some food on the table as well. At that moment my neighbor knocked on the door and said she had made a special dessert that she wanted to share with me. It was an old Russian recipe for strawberries and cream. As she handed me the bowl, I remembered that this had been one of my grandfather's favorite dishes. He had prepared it for me when I was a small child, and in my teen years I had written a poem about it. He had proudly framed the poem and hung it in his den. I thanked my neighbor and took the bowl of strawberries and cream inside. I scooped half onto another plate and put it on the altar. I did a silent meditation and as I ate my portion of the strawberries and cream, I felt the loving presence of my grandfather.

SPELL FOR PSYCHICS

Ingredients

lightbulbs
jasmine tea
blue dish towel

Brew a cup of jasmine tea. Carefully anoint the top of the light-bulb with the tea. Use your pinkie and trace an eye onto the bulb. Let the tea dry and then screw the bulb into a lamp socket. Cover the lamp with a blue dish towel. Blue represents the ocean and all its mystery. Colors of a watery element (blue, turquoise, sea green) are used to increase psychic vibrations. Use this light only when you are doing your spiritual work. The only light more powerful for inducing psychic vibrations is the light of the full moon. Also, drinking jasmine tea before retiring at night can bring prophetic dreams.

SPELL FOR PROPHETIC DREAMS

Ingredients

poppy seed bagel

Poppy is used to induce trances or sleep and to reveal information while in a dream state. Bagels with their round shape and hole in the center symbolize the moon or feminine intuition. Place a poppy seed bagel under your pillow at night. Take a bite first thing in the morning to remember your dream.

SPELL TO SEE THE FUTURE OR PAST

Ingredients

saffron
peppermint

One of the most expensive spices, saffron was once as prized as gold. Make a saffron tea and sip it slowly. Sit by candlelight and gaze into a bowl of water as if it were a crystal ball. This is known as the art of scrying. You must sit until after the eyes begin to tear. After a while the eyes will clear again. This is known as the time of vision. Then your future will be revealed.

To see a past life, drink a cup of peppermint tea and repeat the above procedure.

SPELL FOR THANKSGIVING AND GRATITUDE

The witches' form of thanksgiving involves the making of libations. Before you enjoy any food or drink, simply pour or section off a portion and set it aside for the gods. You will need a bowl or platter in the middle of the table to do this. It is customary to empty the bowl outside under a tree once the meal is completed. This way the food returns to Mother Earth. To give thanks to a particular deity, simply choose a food sacred to that god and place it outdoors. For example, if you have been blessed with love, choose a food sacred to Venus (perhaps an apple) and leave it as an offering to her.

BIBLIOGRAPHY

Boyce, Charles. *Shakespeare A to Z.* New York: Roundtable Press, 1990.

Chia, Mantak, and Maneewan Chia. *Chi Nei Tsang.* New York: Healing Tao Books, 1990.

Culpeper, Nicholas. *Culpeper's Complete Herbal & English Physician.* Illinois: Meyerbooks, 1990.

Cumberlege, Geoffrey (Publisher). *The Oxford Dictionary of Quotations, Second Edition.* New York: Oxford University Press, 1955.

Cunningham, Scott. *Encyclopedia of Magical Herbs.* St. Paul, MN: Llewellyn Publications, 1992.

Cunningham, Scott. *The Magic in Food.* St. Paul, MN: Llewellyn Publications, 1990.

Daley, Mary Dowling. *Irish Laws.* Belfast: Appletree Press Ltd., 1989.

Feliks, Dr. Jehuda. *The Animal World of the Bible.* Israel: Sinai Pub., 1962.

Fielding, William J. *Strange Customs of Courtship and Marriage.* New York: Permabooks, 1949.

Fierz-David, Linda. *Women's Dionysian Initiation: The Villa of Mysteries in Pompeii.* Dallas, Texas: Spring Publications, Inc., 1988.

Bibliography

Guirand, Felix (editor). *New Larousse Encyclopedia of Mythology.* Hong Kong: The Hamlyn Publishing Group Ltd., 1972.

Gurudas. *The Spiritual Properties of Herbs.* San Rafael, CA: Cassandra Press, 1988.

Hand, Wayland D., Anna Cassetta, and Sondra B. Theiderman (editors). *Popular Beliefs and Superstitions: A Compendium of American Folklore.* Boston: G.K. Hall, 1981.

Leach, Maria (editor). *Funk & Wagnalls Standard Dictionary of Folklore, Mythology, and Legend.* San Francisco: Harper & Row, 1984.

McGee, Harold. *On Food and Cooking: The Science and Lore of the Kitchen.* New York: Collier, 1988.

Mickaharic, Draja. *Spiritual Cleansing.* ME: Samuel Weiser Inc., 1982.

Mindell, Earl. *Vitamin Bible.* New York: Warner Books, 1979.

Panati, Charles. *Panati's Extraordinary Origins of Everyday Things.* New York: Harper & Row, 1987.

Patai, Raphael. *The Hebrew Goddess.* Israel: Ktav Publishing House, 1967.

Rätsch, Dr. Christian. *The Dictionary of Sacred and Magical Plants.* Australia: Unity Press, 1992.

Reik, Theodor. *Pagan Rites in Judaism.* New York: The Noonday Press, 1964.

Rose, Donna. *The Magic of Herbs.* Hialeah, FL: Mi-World Pub. Co., 1978.

Rose, Jeanne. *Herbs & Things.* New York: Putnam Publishing Group, 1972.

Slater, Herman (editor). *The Magickal Formulary.* New York: Magickal Childe, Inc., 1981.

Valiente, Doreen. *The Rebirth of Witchcraft.* London: Robert Hale Limited, 1989.

Walker, Barbara. *Woman's Encyclopedia of Myths and Secrets.* San Francisco: Harper & Row, 1983.

Walker, Barbara. *Woman's Encyclopedia of Symbols and Sacred Objects.* San Francisco: Harper Collins Publishers, 1988.

Ward, Bernard. *Healing Foods from the Bible.* New York: Globe Communications Corp., 1994.

Wedeck, Harry and Baskin, Wade. *Dictionary of Pagan Religions.* New Jersey: The Citadel Press, 1973.

MIND MEETS BODY...
HEALTH MEETS HAPPINESS...
SPIRIT MEETS SERENITY...

In his writings, spiritual advisor Edgar Cayce counseled thousands with his extraordinary, yet practical guidance to the mind/body/spirit connection. Now, the Edgar Cayce series, based on actual readings by the renowned psychic, can provide you with insights in the search for understanding and meaning in life.

KEYS TO HEALTH: The Promise and Challenge of Holism
Eric A. Mein, M.D.
_____ 95616-9 $4.99 U.S./$5.99 CAN.

REINCARNATION: Claiming Your Past, Creating Your Future
Lynn Elwell Sparrow
_____ 95754-8 $4.99 U.S./$5.99 CAN.

DREAMS: Tonight's Answers for Tomorrow's Questions
Mark Thurston, Ph.D.
_____ 95771-8 $5.50 U.S./$6.50 CAN.

Publishers Book and Audio Mailing Service
P.O. Box 120159, Staten Island, NY 10312-0004
Please send me the book(s) I have checked above. I am enclosing $_____ (please add $1.50 for the first book, and $.50 for each additional book to cover postage and handling. Send check or money order only—no CODs) or charge my VISA, MASTERCARD, DISCOVER or AMERICAN EXPRESS card.

Card Number_____

Expiration date_____Signature_____

Name_____

Address_____

City_____State/Zip _____
Please allow six weeks for delivery. Prices subject to change without notice. Payment in U.S. funds only. New York residents add applicable sales tax.